Elite • 72

Napoleon's Commanders (1) c1792–1809

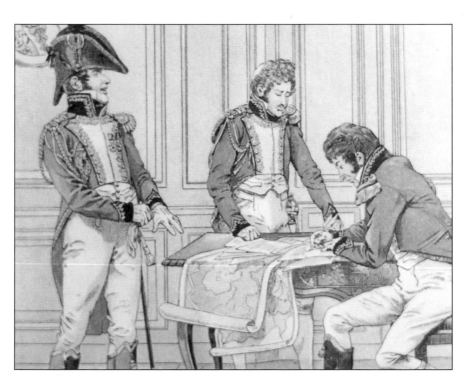

Philip Haythornthwaite • Illustrated by Patrice Courcelle

Series editor Martin Windrow

First published in Great Britain in 2001 by Osprey Publishing,
PO Box 883, Oxford, OX1 9PL, UK
PO Box 3985, New York, NY 10185-3985, USA
Email: info@ospreypublishing.com

Osprey Publishing is part of the Osprey Group.

Transferred to digital print on demand 2014.

First published 2001
1st impression 2001

Printed and bound by
Cadmus Communications, USA.

A CIP catalogue record for this book is available from the
British Library.

ISBN: 978 1 84176 055 1

Editorial by Martin Windrow
Index by Alan Rutter
Design by Ken Vail Graphic Design, Cambridge, UK
Originated by Colourpath, London, UK

The Woodland Trust
Osprey Publishing is supporting the Woodland Trust,
the UK's leading woodland conservation charity, by funding
the dedication of trees.

www.ospreypublishing.com

Author's note
This is the first of two Elite Series titles offering brief
biographies of some of Napoleon's significant subordinates,
and other prominent French commanders of the Revolutionary
and Napoleonic Wars, and illustrating some of the uniforms of
general officers and their staffs.

The present title concentrates upon the period up to 1809,
the forthcoming second volume on subsequent years.
Obviously, this division must be to some extent artificial, given
the long careers of some French commanders: Jean-Baptiste
Jourdan, for example, first commanded an army in September
1793 and was effectively in command of another when he was
defeated at Vittoria almost twenty years later.

Artist's note
Readers may care to note that the original paintings from which
the colour plates in this book were prepared are available for
private sale. All reproduction copyright whatsoever is retained
by the Publishers. All enquiries should be addressed to:

Patrice Courcelle, 33 avenue des Vallons,
1410 Waterloo, Belgium

The Publishers regret that they can enter into no
correspondence upon this matter.

Editor's note
In order to avoid an unmanageable number of italicised phrases
in this text, for the sake of clarity we have instead adopted
English capitalisation of titles and designations – e.g. Duc de
Rivoli, 2e Chasseurs à Cheval, etc.

NAPOLEON'S COMMANDERS (1) c1792–1809

General Marie-Joseph-Paul-Yves-Roch-Gilbert du Motier, Marquis de Lafayette (1757–1834). Most famous for his participation on the Colonial side in the American War of Independence, Lafayette played an important role in the early stages of the French Revolution. As an advocate of a reformed monarchy he was declared a traitor by the more extreme Revolutionary government, and in August 1792 had to leave his command of the Army of the North and seek sanctuary with the Allies. He was permitted to return to France in 1799, but remained an opponent of Napoleon. (Engraving by W.Greatbatch)

INTRODUCTION

Even the most brilliant commander-in-chief is dependent upon his subordinates to carry out his instructions; Napoleon recognised this when in 1806 he remarked that success depended upon the intelligence and courage of generals. This was especially true in larger campaigns, when armies were so increased in size that it became beyond the capacity of even the most gifted commander to supervise all operations in person. Although at times success or failure depended upon the actions of lower-ranking individuals, most responsibility was placed upon those of the rank of general.

More than 2,000 officers achieved this rank in the French army (or the equivalent in the navy) during the French Revolutionary and Napoleonic Wars, but a considerable number of these played only minor roles in the campaigns of the era. There were two ranks of general officer: *général de brigade* and the more senior *général de division*, though the holder was not necessarily the commander of a brigade or division. These ranks were instituted from 21 February 1793 as replacements for the original ranks of *maréchal de camp* and *lieutenant-général* respectively, which terms were thought to have Royalist connotations; they were reinstated upon the Bourbon restoration of 1814. The higher rank of *général d'armée* existed between 1790 and 1793, but later became the appointment of *général en chef*, not a rank as such but applied to the commander of an army. The ancient appointment of *maréchal de France* was abolished in 1793, but was restored by Napoleon – in the form *maréchal de l'Empire* – in 1804; only two of the previous holders survived to that year, the Duc de Broglie (1718–1804) and Rochambeau (1725–1807). Throughout the period, Napoleon appointed only 26 marshals.

One of the best-known of Napoleon's reported remarks was that every French soldier carried the baton of a Marshal of France in his knapsack: in other words, promotion and distinction were available to all who possessed the ability. That is, however, a considerable simplification of what actually occurred.

The effect of the Revolution of 1789 upon the French officer corps was profound. Prior to that event, and especially after 1781, commissioned rank was restricted to those of noble descent, which stifled the opportunities for advancement of those from the middle classes and of deserving 'other ranks'. (There were exceptions, however, and the interpretation of 'nobility' was perhaps wider than in some countries: for example, Napoleon's Marshal Philibert Sérurier, who was first commissioned at the age of 13, was usually regarded as a member of the minor nobility although his father was only a small landowner and

General Charles-François Dumouriez (1739–1823), best remembered for his 'treason'. As an officer of the old Royal army he supported the French Revolution, served as foreign minister, won the victory of Jemappes and shared that of Valmy with Kellermann (qv). Fearing the extremist Revolutionaries, however, he intrigued with the Austrians, and when his plans failed he fled to them. He continued to be involved in Royalist agitation, and finally became an adviser to the British government; he died in England. (Engraving by W.Greatbach)

mole-catcher in the king's service). This system was swept away by the Revolution, and so was a large proportion of the existing officer corps – by the emigration of Royalists unwilling to support the new régime, and by purges against those who remained but who were considered insufficiently zealous in their support for Republican ideals. The latter was an important consideration: from the beginning of the Revolutionary Wars to the fall of the Directory, more than 72 per cent of generals holding a command were disciplined, mostly for political reasons, and no fewer than 55 were executed. For example, the Armée du Nord was especially unfortunate with its commanders in just a single year (1792–93): two fled for their lives to the enemy (Lafayette and Dumouriez), one was killed in battle (Dampierre), two were guillotined (Custine and Houchard) and two were arrested briefly (Lamarche – a temporary appointment – and Kilmaine). Lafayette's predecessor in command was executed in 1794 (Luckner).

Nevertheless, a considerable number of nobles remained in the army, even if, like Davout, they thought it advisable to change the spelling of their name (in his case from the more 'aristocratic' d'Avout) – though not even the adoption of the name 'Egalité' saved the Duc d'Orléans from the guillotine. To replace those officers who had emigrated or been cashiered, and to provide more for the enlarged army of the Revolutionary Wars, many experienced members of the 'other ranks' were promoted, so that the influence of the old Royal army remained considerable: for example, eight of Napoleon's 26 marshals had been officers under the Ancien Régime, and no fewer than ten had originally served in the ranks. Some sixteen years after the Revolution, of generals who held commands in the Austerlitz campaign, about 65 per cent seem to have served in the old Royal army, about 22 per cent as officers (two had even been pages to the king), and about 5 per cent had served in foreign armies before the Revolution. Even seven years later, of the generals who held commands at Borodino about 31 per cent had served in the Royal army, about 14 per cent as officers (including two in the navy), and three had served in foreign armies at that time.

In some of the units created in the early stages of the Revolutionary Wars officers were elected by their fellows, which could lead to very rapid promotion. Marshal Massena, for instance, went from NCO to lieutenant-colonel by election; on the strength of two years' military service, Oudinot was elected straight to captain; and Lannes was elected an officer on the same day that he enlisted. The case of Marshal Laurent Gouvion St Cyr shows the possible rapidity of promotion: an artist with no practical military experience, he enlisted as a private on 1 September 1792 and attained the highest rank possible as *général de division* provisionally in June 1794.

Such circumstances led to some individuals achieving a rank for which they were unfit, even some generals being barely literate or incapable of understanding a map. Nevertheless, the majority who rose to command in the Revolutionary period were men of some education and military experience (even if only in the ranks), or with a family tradition of military service. Of Napoleon's marshals, excluding the one genuine foreigner (Poniatowski, a Polish prince), one was a marquis in his own right (Grouchy) and at least five more (six if Sérurier is included) came from upper-class families. Only five were of genuinely humble origin, and the remainder from the professional or lower middle classes. Even so, the difference between old and new systems was profound. Before the Revolution it was necessary for a candidate officer to prove four 'quarterings of nobility' in his ancestry, but other considerations prevailed thereafter, exemplified by Napoleon's remark to Marbot: when Marbot said that he had suffered eight wounds, Napoleon remarked that he had eight quarterings of nobility as a consequence!

Experience of life in the lower ranks, or at least a knowledge of the lot of the ordinary soldier, could have advantages. For example, General Antoine Laroche-Dubouscat, who had enlisted as a dragoon in 1774,

Marshal Jean-Mathieu-Philibert Sérurier (1742–1819), one of Napoleon's earliest and staunchest subordinates in the Army of Italy. After a long career as a regimental officer in the Royal army he attained general rank in 1793; his active career ended in 1799, and his appointment to the marshalate in 1804 was largely honorary. Although not the most brilliant of talents he was an honest man of unblemished reputation; Napoleon commented that Sérurier always retained the manners and severity of an old major of infantry. (Engraving after J.L.Laneuville)

once assembled a regiment when no trumpeter was available by blowing the trumpet-call himself – a skill he had learned as a boy. Such factors could also increase an officer's prestige amongst his men. An example of this was General Henry-Antoine Jardon, who, although having begun his military career as an officer in Netherlands service in 1789, was called 'the voltigeur general', marched with his troops musket in hand, and shared their bivouacs, which made him very popular. (He was killed by a Portuguese peasant at Negrelos in March 1809.)

Previous military experience, however, did not necessarily make for a competent general: for example, three of the generals condemned by Napoleon as unfit to command even a battalion, when he first took over the Army of Italy, appear to have had a combined military service of 60 years. Some of those who became generals had unlikely skills: for example, Jean-François Carteaux, who commanded at the siege of Toulon, had left the army in 1779 and had become court painter to Louis XVI. (Other generals with similar abilities included Louis-François Lejeune, one of the best of all military painters; while Jean-Baptiste Francheschi-Delonne, perhaps best-known as the leader of a light cavalry division in the Corunna campaign, and who died in Spanish captivity in 1810, was an expert sculptor.) Jean-Antoine Rossignol, a notable commander in the war in the Vendée, had left the army in 1783 to become a jeweller; his renewed military career was not a success, and ended when Napoleon deported him to the Seychelles in 1801.

Foreign origins

A considerable number of foreigners rose to high rank. Of the Napoleonic marshals, for example, Poniatowski was from Poland (the cradle of a number of significant commanders), Massena was born at Nice at a time when that place was Piedmontese, Macdonald's father was

General François-Séverin Marceau-Desgraviers (1769–96) was one of the most famous 'fallen heroes' of the Revolutionary Wars. A stormer of the Bastille who became a general in 1793, this friend of Kléber (qv) served in the Vendée, notably at Fleurus, and in Germany with Jourdan and Kléber. He was mortally wounded by an Austrian sharpshooter at Altenkirchen on 19 September 1796 and died in Austrian hands two days later. Such was the Austrians' respect for Marceau that in an example of old-fashioned chivalry the Archduke Charles ordered that his body be returned with all due ceremony, and both French and Austrian artillery fired mourning salutes. The coffin is shown here dressed with his plumed hat, sash and sword, carried on a black-draped wagon or caisson under Austrian escort. (Engraving by Sergent-Marceau) a Jacobite exile from Scotland (the marshal spoke no English but could converse in Gaelic), Kellermann was from Alsace and of distant German ancestry, Augereau was half-German, and Mortier was half-English (so that each could speak the language of their mother as well as French). Jacques-Alexandre-Bernard Law, Marquis de Lauriston, one of several French generals born in India, was great-nephew of the famous financier in France, John Law of Lauriston, near Edinburgh. Many of Irish and Scots origin had served in the Royal army, notably in the Irish regiments, and were generals in the early Revolutionary Wars, such as the brothers Arthur and Theobald Dillon (the former guillotined, the latter murdered in the Revolution), Isidore Lynch and Dominic Sheldon (born in London and Winchester respectively), and Napoleon's early cavalry commander Charles Kilmaine. The Irish rebellion of 1798 brought into French service (without much military success) the noted Irish political leaders James Napper Tandy and Arthur O'Connor, both of whom were commissioned as generals.

Generals of German origin included Charles, Prince of Isemburg (colonel of the foreign regiment of the French army which bore his name), and Prince Heinrich of Reuss-Schleitz, killed in Saxony in 1813. The Netherlands provided many more generals, including some not ancestrally native to that area, like David Bruce, who served in the Peninsula (another Dutch general of the same name served against the British expedition to Walcheren). Switzerland also provided a number, perhaps the most famous being Jean-Louis Reynier and Antoine-Henri Jomini. A number came from the Americas, including some born in French colonies; they included at least one ex-plantation slave and the remarkable Toussaint L'Ouverture, *général de division* in French service, who became head of state in Haiti until arrested and left to die in a French prison. Generals from the United States included George Rogers Clark, brother of the explorer William Clark, who had played a considerable part in the American War of Independence and was appointed a French *général de brigade* in 1793 in preparation for an abortive attack on Spanish possessions west of the Mississippi; and John Eustace, who had also served in the US Army during the War of Independence and was on Luckner's staff in 1792. Jean-Antoine Milfort was of French birth and had served in the French army, but had also been a chief of the Creek nation, fighting against the Americans.

For and against

A number of French generals served against France at some period of their career. Some were early émigrés, like François Jarry, who after long service in Prussia became a general under Luckner but emigrated in 1792, and subsequently was influential in helping to establish the first system of higher education for officers of the British Army. Another Royalist émigré was Hippolyte-Marie-Guillaume Piré, who had a distinguished career as a cavalry commander in Napoleon's army, culminating at Waterloo; in 1794–95 he had served against the French as a member of Rohan's Legion in

Louis-Lazare Hoche (1768–97), thought by Napoleon to have been one of France's best generals. His greatest successes were probably in the suppression of the rebellion in the Vendée – which he achieved with unusual humanity – and, in command of the Army of the Sambre & Meuse, in his victory at Neuweid (18 April 1797). His career was interrupted by unfounded accusations of complicity in the treasons of Dumouriez and Pichegru; his sudden death at the age of 29 on 19 September 1797 aroused suspicions of poisoning, but the cause was probably consumption. Hoche exemplified those of little education who could rise to high rank through innate ability; his ADC, Lejeune, noted that he 'could only just read and sign his name, but he was a fine fellow, and his courage was indomitable'. (Engraving by W.Greatbach)

British service. Another distinguished French officer was Nicolas-François Roussel d'Hurbal, who had served in the Austrian army from 1782; he rose to the rank of *Generalmajor*, fought with distinction at Aspern-Essling, and led a cuirassier brigade at Wagram. After fighting against the French for so long, but becoming unemployed after the 1809 campaign, he was appointed as a general in Napoleon's army in 1811 and served there with equal distinction, being wounded at Borodino, the Katzbach and Waterloo. The Venezuelan-born Francesco Miranda, who served with distinction as a general in the French army in 1792–93, later devoted his energies towards the independence of Spain's South American colonies, and was responsible for providing a considerable opponent to the French in the Peninsula by recommending Thomas Picton to Wellington.

Bernadotte and Moreau are the best-known of those who changed sides after long careers in the French army, and both consequently attracted criticism. A story in this regard told how Moreau was said to have remarked to Jomini that it was curious that they, ex-French generals, should now both be in Russian service and opposed to France. Jomini pointedly replied that there was a difference between them: he was not a Frenchman! Others fought against Napoleon more from changes in political rather than personal circumstances: for example, following the establishment of the independent kingdom of the Netherlands, among the senior officers of that state who fought against Napoleon at Waterloo were David Chassé, Charles Anthing and

Jean-Baptiste Van Merlen, all of whom had earlier been generals in Napoleon's army.

Among the large number of officers who attained the rank of general in the French army during the Revolutionary and Napoleonic period a considerable number were of little military significance, and some appointments were motivated largely by political considerations. Others held active appointments as generals only briefly. For example, the Corsican leader Pascal Paoli was a French general for a short time, while Paul Barras, the corrupt politician and head of the Directory, was also commissioned as a general even though his practical military experience was limited to service at Pondicherry and had ended in 1786.

The rewards

Frederick the Great remarked that military command gave men an 'opportunity for acquiring glory, rescuing their names from the rust of oblivion, and securing by their brilliant actions a glorious and immortal fame'[1], but it was not necessary to become a general to achieve this. A touching story was told of Jean-Baptiste Sourd, colonel of the 2e Chevau-Légers-Lanciers, who at Genappe in 1815 received several sabre-cuts, treatment of which required the amputation of his right arm. As the famous surgeon Larrey performed the operation Sourd dictated a note to Napoleon, declining promotion to general as he preferred to remain in command of his regiment; when the amputation was completed he signed the note with his left hand and rode off to rejoin his men.

In addition to prestige, great financial rewards could be accumulated by those who attained the higher ranks; peerages might be accompanied by the income from estates, and grants in cash could be substantial, while some took the opportunity to enrich themselves by more irregular means. Often, however, the rewards were hard-won, for the rank of general could prove hazardous to hold. For example, it appears that of the Napoleonic marshals only Sérurier was not injured during the French Revolutionary and Napoleonic Wars (though he had been shot in the jaw at Warburg in 1760), while Oudinot received at least 22 wounds during his career. Eight of the marshals died violently: three in battle (including one drowned), two executed, two murdered, and one probably by an accident.

A story exemplifying the point was told of Marshal Lefebvre, whose military career enabled him to acquire riches otherwise unattainable by one from his humble background. A friend being entertained at his mansion appeared jealous of the marshal's wealth: 'I see you are envious of what I have', said Lefebvre; 'well, you shall have these things at a better bargain than I had. Come into the court[yard]; I'll fire at you with a gun twenty times, at thirty paces, and if I don't kill you, all this shall be yours.' 'You won't', was the reply. 'Very well', said the marshal; 'recollect, then, that I have been shot at more than a thousand times, and from much closer, before I arrived where you find me.'[2]

A French general (left), wearing a tricolour sash and separate red, white and blue hat plumes; and an ADC, whose light blue brassard worn with what seems to be a regimental uniform shows him to be an aide to a *général de brigade*. Although this watercolour by J.A.Langendyk, dated 1803, is not accurate in all details (e.g. it was not usual for general officers to wear gorgets), it portrays the general appearance of staff officers of the late Revolutionary Wars. (The Royal Collection © 2000 HM Queen Elizabeth II)

BIOGRAPHIES

AUGEREAU, Maréchal Charles-Pierre-François, Duc de Castiglione (1757–1816)

The son of a Parisian fruit-seller, Pierre Augereau (**see Plate F**) exemplified the opportunities for advancement made possible by the French Revolution. Enlisting as a private soldier in 1774, he established a reputation as a champion swordsman and duellist, but fled the army after killing an officer in a quarrel. At least by his own account, he then led a wandering life of considerable adventure; he claimed to have served in the Russian army, and certainly did join the Prussian army, but deserted again to ply a trade as a dancing- and fencing-master until an amnesty for deserters permitted him to rejoin the French army. Commissioned in 1792 and a *général de division* in the following year, he must have presented a marked contrast with the often shabby appearance of much of the army: nicknamed *'le grand Prussien'* ('the big Prussian'), he was meticulous in his dress and appearance, and always insistent upon discipline and drill. He was one of Napoleon's principal subordinates in Italy (the young General Bonaparte, as he then was, reported that he was brave, popular, steady and lucky), and won his greatest distinction at Castiglione, from where he took the name of his dukedom when it was awarded in 1808. His own account may have exaggerated his contribution to the victory, but nevertheless in later years Napoleon never forgot that 'he saved us at Castiglione'.

Augereau gained a reputation for avarice: Napoleon stated that his manners and language remained those of a bravo, which he was far from being, when 'sated with honours and riches, which he had bestowed upon himself on every occasion that offered, and by every means in his power'[(3)]; but Marmont remarked that he seemed to derive almost as much pleasure from giving away money as he did from acquiring it, and his ADC Marbot remarked that no man was ever more generous or ready to do a kindness.

One of the original marshals, Augereau led VII Corps in 1805, at Jena, and at Eylau – where he was so ill that he had to be held in his saddle rather than abandon his duty (and was wounded in the arm by a grapeshot and bruised by his falling horse). A capable tactician if perhaps less competent handling larger formations, his abilities seem to have declined with age and ill-health, though he led the Army of Catalonia in 1809, served in Germany in 1812 and at Leipzig. His bravery was acknowledged, but Napoleon remarked that he 'seemed to

Charles Pierre-François Augereau, Duc de Castiglione. Augereau was one of the few commanders whose active career encompassed virtually the entire Napoleonic era; he was a senior and much more experienced general in the Army of Italy before Bonaparte arrived to take command in March 1796, and despite increasing ill-health he continued to hold important commands until 1814. (Print after Delpech) be tired and disheartened by victory, of which he always had enough'[(4)]. Despite his sterling conduct at Leipzig, Macdonald claimed that subsequently Augereau was very critical of Napoleon: 'That idiot does not know what he is about... he has completely lost his head ... The coward! He abandoned and was prepared to sacrifice us all; but do you imagine that I am fool enough to let myself be killed or made prisoner for the sake of a Leipsic suburb? You should have done as I did, and have gone away!'[(5)]. In 1814 Augereau commanded the Army of the Rhône, but his conduct was sluggish and he abandoned Lyons to the enemy – to Napoleon's fury. He declared his allegiance to the Bourbons; this preserved his position at the First Restoration, but he attempted to rejoin Napoleon in 1815, was rebuffed, and after the Hundred Days was understandably mistrusted by the king. He was dismissed, and died at his estate at La Houssaye on 12 June 1816.

BERNADOTTE, Maréchal Jean-Baptiste-Jules, Prince de Ponte Corvo (1763–1844)

It is perhaps ironic that of all Napoleon's commanders and the Imperial family, the only one to create an enduring royal dynasty was Bernadotte (see Plate H), originally an ardent Republican. The son of a lawyer from Pau in Gascony, Jean-Baptiste was also intended for the legal profession but instead enlisted as a private soldier in the army, in 1780. His abilities were recognised and by 1788 he was a sergeant-major, so noted for his immaculate appearance that he was nicknamed *'sergent Belle-Jambe'* ('sergeant pretty-legs'). He was commissioned in 1791, and a combination of talent and devotion to the Republic led to rapid promotion: field officer by February 1794, *général de brigade* in June and *de division* by October of that year. Distinguished while commanding a division of the Army of the Sambre & Meuse in 1795–96, he came to Napoleon's notice with the Army of Italy in 1797. Although co-operation between them was not always easy, he became linked to the Bonaparte family by his marriage in 1798 to Désirée Clary, Joseph Bonaparte's sister-in-law. Bernadotte had an unfortunate experience as ambassador to Vienna, where overt Republicans were not very welcome, but he later served as minister of war and, despite declining to help Napoleon with the *coup d'état* of Brumaire, he was among the first creations of the marshalate in 1804.

In 1805 Bernadotte led I Corps and played a leading role in the victory of Austerlitz, and in June 1806 was rewarded with the title of Prince of Ponte Corvo. This was probably the highpoint of his career

Augereau in the *grand uniforme* of a marshal, with the cape, elaborately feathered hat, breeches and stockings worn for court dress or occasions of the greatest ceremony – *'grande costume de gala'* – see Plate F3; Augereau was renowned for his immaculate dress at all times. Desaix (qv) describes him as a large, handsome man with a big nose; and also as having few equals as a soldier, but always bragging. He tended to overstate his role at Castiglione, although Napoleon admitted that it had been very important. (Engraving by T.Johnson after R.Lefevre)

under French colours, for in the Jena campaign he was censured for the slowness of his advance; he missed Eylau when despatches went astray; and in June 1807 he was shot in the neck at Spanden. In the following month he was appointed governor of the Hanseatic towns, but led IX Corps in the 1809 Danube campaign. After being criticised for the performance of his command at Wagram he left the army. Subsequently given command of the force intended to oppose the British landing at Walcheren, Bernadotte was criticised further by Napoleon, who suggested that he was intriguing to restore the Republic, and he was relieved of all duties.

There his career might have ended, had he not shown kindness to Swedish prisoners in the late war. This was remembered when an heir was sought for the childless King Charles XIII of that country, and although Napoleon thought the proposal absurd he raised no objection, having no further use for Bernadotte's services. Changing his name to Charles-Jean and his religion to Lutheran, Bernadotte was elected as Crown Prince of Sweden on 21 August 1810. In this capacity he joined the Sixth Coalition against Napoleon and led the Army of the North in 1813–14, winning the battles of Grossbeeren and Dennewitz and playing a significant role at Leipzig. Suggestions that he entertained hopes of succeeding Napoleon as ruler of France were never realistic, as most Frenchmen regarded him as a traitor: Marbot, for example, stated that he had only achieved a throne by the glory won at the head of French troops, and that he then proceeded to show ingratitude to his country. Napoleon also criticised him, stating that if Bernadotte had supported France against Russia he might have held the fate of the world in his hands, but instead 'he was swayed by personal considerations, silly vanity, and all sorts of mean passions. His head was turned, when he saw that he, an old Jacobin, was courted and flattered by legitimates; when he found himself holding political and friendly conferences face to face with an Emperor of all the Russias... he sacrificed both his new and his mother country, his own glory, his true power, the cause of the people, the welfare of Europe'[6].

For all Napoleon's invective, however, in February 1818 Bernadotte became King Charles XIV of Sweden (Carl XIV Johan), and proved a moderate and kindly ruler who unified Sweden and Norway, though latterly he was criticised for his conservatism by liberal factions. Upon his death he was succeeded by his son, King Oscar I; and the Bernadotte dynasty still survives on the Swedish throne, commemorating one of the most remarkable of Napoleon's commanders.

Jean-Baptiste-Jules Bernadotte, Marshal of the Empire and Prince of Ponte Corvo. This portrait shows him in his slightly later role as Crown Prince of Sweden, wearing the Swedish Order of the Seraphim (or 'blue ribbon') and Order of the Sword ('yellow ribbon') conferred upon him in 1810. It was perhaps unusual that so ardent a Republican should found a royal dynasty; Napoleon referred to him as 'the only upstart sovereign in Europe' – ironically enough, considering the emperor's own path to the throne. (Print after Delpech)

Bernadotte in the uniform of a marshal, his triumphs symbolised by the captured enemy colour resting across the mortar at his side. The coat is that of the dress uniform (see Plate H1), without the additional gold embroidery upon the seams of the *grand uniforme* used for ceremonial occasions. Other indications of rank include the baton bearing imperial eagles, and the crossed batons device on the knot of the sash's tasselled end. (Engraving by T.Johnson after F.Kinson)

BERTHIER, Maréchal Louis-Alexandre, Prince de Neuchâtel et de Wagram (1753–1815)

None of Napoleon's subordinates can have been more important to him than Louis Berthier **(see Plate K)**, for although he rarely led troops in the field he was invaluable as one of the first professional staff officers. Born at Versailles, he began his career as a military engineer like his father, but very soon undertook staff duties, notably with Rochambeau in the American War of Independence. In the early Revolutionary period he commanded the Versailles National Guard for a short time (helping in the escape of Louis XVI's aunts) before resuming staff duties

Louis-Alexandre Berthier, in a relatively early portrait showing the 1796 uniform of a *général de division*, which rank he had attained in June 1795 – cf Plate A2. The shattered bridge behind him recalls the battle of Lodi, where he was among a number of senior officers who led the second, successful attempt to storm across the river under heavy fire. Although best remembered for his invaluable staff work, Berthier was never lacking in courage when the occasion demanded. (Engraving by H.Davidson after Gros)

under Rochambeau, Lafayette and Luckner (as *maréchal de camp* from 1792). Suspended briefly because of his Royalist background, he was reinstated and sent as chief of staff to Napoleon in Italy. The latter's early evaluation of Berthier was accurate: a man of courage, activity, talent and character in the role for which he was ideally suited. Although at times he held field commands, he had little skill in that direction; Napoleon remarked, somewhat unkindly, that 'Nature has evidently designed many for a subordinate situation; and among these is Berthier. As a chief of staff he had no superior; but he was not fit to command five hundred men'[7].

His abilities in putting Napoleon's instructions into practice, however, were huge; his tireless work and attention to detail made him extremely effective in administering the large and complex staff system, which expanded as armies increased in size and operated over wider areas. Berthier also served as minister of war (1799–1800 and 1800–07); and was in nominal command of the Army of Reserve in the Marengo campaign (Napoleon being excluded officially from command as First Consul), where he was wounded in the arm.

He was among the first creation of the marshalate in 1804, became Prince of Neuchâtel in March 1806 and – though his failings in tactical matters were again demonstrated at the beginning of the 1809 campaign – Prince of Wagram in August 1809. Throughout the campaigns he was at Napoleon's side, transmitting his orders and turning his plans into reality, and controlling with great skill the various staff departments which administered the army. He was left behind temporarily when Napoleon abandoned the remains of the Russian expedition in 1812, but was back with Imperial headquarters for the 1813–14 campaigns, in which he suffered a lance-wound in the head at Brienne. Vital though he was to Napoleon's conduct of campaigns, and although Napoleon regarded him as a friend, the emperor may never have appreciated Berthier's true value, once describing him as merely a 'chief clerk'. Napoleon was even capable of assaulting him physically; and Marbot believed that Berthier so came to dread Napoleon's outbursts of fury that it inhibited his natural talents and stifled his initiative, as he merely followed orders rather than making suggestions.

Berthier's devotion to duty was total, but he claimed to be over-worked to the point of death and apparently became somewhat morose, especially after Napoleon arranged for him a marriage with Princess Marie-Elisabeth of Bavaria (March 1808) instead of to his beloved mistress, Madame Visconti. Her husband died shortly after Berthier's wedding, whereupon he was said to have bemoaned his 'miserable condition... with a little more constancy, Madame Visconti might have been my wife'[8].

After Napoleon's first abdication he supported the Bourbons, and remained loyal to the king upon Napoleon's return in 1815. The absence of one who had worked for him so diligently for so many years must have been felt keenly by Napoleon in the Hundred Days campaign; but Berthier never saw the final defeat of his old master. On 1 June 1815 he fell to his death from a window at Bamberg, in somewhat mysterious circumstances; it was probably just an accident, although suspicions were understandably aroused of either murder or suicide, the latter prompted by the fact that when he fell Berthier was watching the passing of Russian troops en route to invade France.

Berthier in his most familiar role as chief of staff, wearing the aiguillette of his appointment as *Major-Général* of the *Grande Armée* (not a rank as such); cf Plate K1. One of the most able of professional staff officers, Berthier was painstaking and dedicated, and not always as highly appreciated as he deserved. On one occasion he was found in tears, complaining that he was being worked to death, and that the lot of the ordinary soldier was preferable to his burdens. Desaix described him as always busy and (intriguingly) always laughing, but the pressure of work no doubt cost him some of his previous good humour – Laure Junot recorded that he chewed his fingernails until they bled. (Engraving by G.Dorrington after M.Jacque)

A marshal or divisional general (right) receives an order carried by one of Berthier's aides, who wears the striking uniform designed by Louis Lejeune: red shako, white dolman and black pelissse. The uniform is like that shown in Plate K2 but with the perhaps more common red trousers with a black stripe instead of the hussar breeches of Lejeune's self-portrait. Lejeune described this uniform as the most brilliant in the army, though it was rather too conspicuous in action. (Engraving after F.Philippoteaux)

BESSIÈRES, Maréchal Jean-Baptiste, Duc d'Istrie (1768–1813)

If somewhat limited as a commander, Jean-Baptiste Bessières **(see Plate J)** was popular and remembered as a man of great humanity, culture and complete honesty. The son of a surgeon, he was intended for the medical profession himself until the French Revolution intervened, and he became a captain in his local National Guard. From there he stepped down in rank to join the king's Constitutional Guard as an ordinary soldier (1792), but rose through the ranks to become an officer again in February 1793. In the Army of Italy he encountered his boyhood friend Joachim Murat, and so entered Napoleon's circle, becoming commander of his Guides and serving with distinction in Italy and Egypt. He assisted in the *coup* of Brumaire and led the Guard cavalry at Marengo, becoming *général de brigade* in July 1800 and *de division* in September 1802. In 1804 he was among the first to be appointed a marshal, despite never having commanded even a medium-sized force in the field, and in the same year became colonel-general of the Imperial Guard cavalry.

Jean-Baptiste Bessières, Duc d'Istrie, one of the most loyal of Napoleon's marshals; see Plate J1. A good commander of cavalry, he was perhaps too cautious when leading larger formations, but he appeared absolutely fearless in action. When covering the withdrawal from the Aspern-Essling bridgehead, following heavy losses and the death of Lannes, he encouraged the troops by calmly walking up and down the forward skirmish line, hands behind his back, under heavy fire. Bessières was immediately recognisable by his long, powdered hair; to some this seemed characteristic of the old-fashioned virtues which he was believed to uphold. (Engraving by Hopwood)

Perhaps the dominant feature of Bessières' personality was his loyalty and integrity, described by Napoleon as of the 'antique' mould: 'kind, humane, and generous... an honest, worthy man'[9], who used his high rank to perform acts of kindness. Devoutly religious, he held old-fashioned ideals which were perhaps visible in his appearance, for he wore his hair powdered long after that style had gone out of fashion (though it was retained by the Guard). Although personally brave, Bessières was not especially distinguished in independent command, suffering from over-caution, though he was a capable subordinate. He led the Guard cavalry in a vital charge at Austerlitz and was distinguished at Eylau; in the Peninsula he won the battle of Medina del Rio Seco but was criticised for lack of drive, and reverted from an independent command to control of the cavalry in the Corunna campaign. He impressed greatly by his calmness in commanding the rearguard at Aspern-Essling, but on the first night of the battle his bitter and long-standing feud with Lannes (under whose orders he had been placed) would have led to violence had not Massena intervened.

Bessières was rewarded with the dukedom of Istria in the week following the battle; succeeded Bernadotte in command of the forces opposing the Walcheren expedition; and in 1811 returned to Spain as head of the Army of the North, where he received some criticism for his caution at Fuentes de Oñoro. While leading the Guard cavalry in Russia in 1812 he was blamed by some for persuading Napoleon not to commit the Guard at Borodino – which, if true, would correspond to the caution he displayed on other occasions. Within the Guard, however, Bessières was adored: when he was knocked from his horse at Wagram a groan rose from the Guardsmen who witnessed it. Bessières was less fortunate subsequently: at Rippach near Weissenfels on 1 May 1813 – the day before the battle of Lützen – he was struck down while reconnoitring by a ricocheting roundshot which caused ghastly and almost immediately fatal injury. Las Cases recalled that Bessières may have had a presentiment of death, since he had remarked shortly beforehand that he hoped they would meet again, 'but at the present crisis, with our young soldiers, we leaders must not spare ourselves'. It was later remarked that he died not far from the spot where Gustavus Adolphus of Sweden was killed in battle in 1632.

Napoleon mourned the loss of a dear friend, though Bessières had been no sycophant; indeed, his honest and forthright opinions had made for an uneasy relationship at times. Las Cases remarked that 'after living like Bayard, he died like Turenne', though Bessières was not exactly *'le chevalier sans peur et sans reproche'* ('the knight without fear and beyond reproach') as Bayard was described. In Spain he was not averse to the shooting of hostages, and though he had what appeared to be a happy marriage, after his death it was revealed that he had been conducting an affair with a chorus girl in the Paris Opera. Given his caution and limits as a general, neither was the comparison with Turenne appropriate in anything but the manner of his death. Napoleon felt his death as deeply as that of his other friend, Duroc, and intended to raise monuments to them both, but was prevented by circumstances; but as Las Cases observed, 'History, whose pages are far more imperishable than marble or bronze, has consecrated them, and secured them for ever from oblivion'[11].

Napoleon and his staff at Wagram, 1809 – the moment when Bessières was unhorsed, causing the greatest consternation among the Guard. Napoleon told him that 'the ball which struck you drew tears from all my Guard. Return thanks to it; it ought to be very dear to you'[10]. Also visible here are members of Napoleon's escort of Chasseurs à Cheval of the Guard, including one (right) carrying his mapcase; and (on foot) one of the imperial pages, wearing the dark green imperial livery with gold lace, and carrying the emperor's telescope slung on his back. (Engraving after Horace Vernet)

Louis Bonaparte as King of Holland, wearing the white uniform then characteristic of troops of that state – see Plate E2. The blue ribbon worn beneath the coat is that of the Royal Order of Merit founded by Louis in 1806, and united in 1808 with his Royal Order of the Union. Its badge consisted of a crowned, eight-armed, white-enamelled cross with the Bonaparte symbol of gold bees between the arms, with a gilt central disc bearing a profile portrait of Louis, surrounded by a green enamel circlet inscribed *'Lodewijk Koning van Holland'*. (Engraving by William Miller after Charles Hodges)

BONAPARTE, Louis, Roi de la Hollande (1778–1846)

Three of Napoleon's brothers attained the rank of general in the French army, but the third, Louis (**see Plate E**), was the one who had the longest military career. Trained as a gunner from 1790, he was commissioned in 1794 and accompanied Napoleon as his aide in Italy and Egypt. Louis joined the 5e Dragons in 1799 and was promoted to *général de brigade* in March 1803, and *de division* a year later. To a considerable extent his life was controlled by Napoleon, who in 1802 arranged for Louis an unfortunate marriage to Hortense Beauharnais, Josephine's daughter; and in 1806 pushed him into the position of King of Holland, a task for which Louis was unenthusiastic. (In this role he commanded both the troops of this new kingdom, and the French forces stationed there.) Once established, Louis proved a rather better king than Napoleon had envisaged: he behaved well towards his subjects, and relations with Napoleon grew strained when he first refused the kingdom of Spain (which therefore was given to their eldest brother, Joseph), and then declined to implement the Continental System on the grounds that the maritime blockade would ruin his subjects.

Napoleon's solution to the conflict was to annex the Kingdom of Holland (9 July 1810) and incorporate it into France. He blamed Louis and his wife, stating that the former had been spoiled by reading Rousseau, had 'whimsical humours' and was 'teazing in his temper', and that had Hortense followed Louis to Holland, and 'had she known how to repress her temper', 'Louis would not then have fled from Amsterdam; and I should not have been compelled to unite his kingdom to mine, a measure which contributed to ruin my credit in Europe'[12]. Following his abdication Louis fled abroad, to Bohemia, Switzerland and finally to Italy – where he settled, using the name of the Comte de St Leu, and was probably much happier than he had been ruling his unwanted kingdom. His son Charles Napoleon Louis (1808–73) became the Emperor Napoleon III.

CARNOT, Général Lazare-Nicolas-Marguerite (1753–1823)

Although not a *général de division* until 1814, few individuals made quite such a mark upon the French army as Lazare Carnot, one of the most influential personalities of the Revolutionary period. A Burgundian of middle-class background, and an engineer officer from 1773, he was an enthusiastic supporter of the Revolution and through his political career exercised an influence on military affairs far beyond his lowly rank (he was only a captain until March 1795, when he became *chef de bataillon*). As a member of the early Revolutionary administration (he was a member of the Committee of Public Safety from August 1793) he was responsible for most military affairs as a combination of minister of war and chief of staff, and presided over the institution of the *levée en masse* and the *amalgame*. Unlike some political appointees who interfered in military affairs, Carnot was a capable man, who visited the armies in person (he contributed considerably to the victory of Wattignies); and from his reforms and administration his nickname, 'the organiser of victory', was well-justified. Indeed, the French army which Napoleon inherited was to a considerable extent the product of Carnot's work.

Appointed a Director in 1795, he was compelled to go into exile in 1797, but returned after the *coup* of Brumaire. In 1800 he served as minister of war, but as a Republican he came into conflict with Napoleon, and in 1801 retired, though he remained a senator (and received a pension from Napoleon). He wrote and worked on scientific pursuits, and at Napoleon's behest produced a very influential book on military engineering for the engineer school at Metz, *De la Défense des Places Fortes* (1810), which came to be used throughout Europe.

'The organiser of victory' – Lazare-Nicolas-Marguerite Carnot. His efforts in reforming the army during the early Revolutionary Wars had a great influence on the quality of the troops inherited by Napoleon, who described him as hard-working, honest, and a stranger to intrigue. Carnot was one of the leading political figures of the 1790s, and his grandson Marie also achieved the highest office: he was the French president assassinated by an Italian anarchist in 1894. (Engraving by J.Massard, showing Carnot during the Revolutionary period)

Carnot wearing the uniform of *général de division*, with three rank stars on the pad of the epaulette, while governor of Antwerp, to which post he was appointed in January 1814. He distinguished himself in this role, as was appropriate for the author of a very influential treatise on the defence of fortified places. Having opposed the creation of the Empire, he was nevertheless one of those who advocated continuing support for Napoleon at its end. (Engraving by R.G.Tietze after Lejeune)

Although he had opposed the creation of the Empire, in the emergency of 1814 he offered his services, and conducted a splendid defence as governor of Antwerp. Even though he was a political opponent, Napoleon said that he 'displayed on every occasion great moral courage' and was 'faithful, laborious, full of probity, and always sincere'[13]. Having been present at the beginning of the Napoleonic era, Carnot was prominent at its close: he served as minister of the interior during the Hundred Days and continued to advocate support of the war, and of Napoleon, after Waterloo. When this became impossible, he was one of the five members of the Executive Commission which assumed control from Napoleon. Proscribed by the Bourbons, he went into exile in 1815 and died at Magdeburg.

The death of Auguste de Colbert at Cacabellos, 3 January 1809, during the Corunna campaign. He was shot while leading a charge against the British rearguard, by Thomas Plunket, a noted 'character' and marksman of the 95th Rifles, who used the prone firing position. Edward Costello, who knew Plunket but was not present, claimed that Plunket was responding to an offer of a purse of money to anyone who would shoot the daring Frenchman made by Sir Edward Paget, but such a base motive was later denied! (Print after Harry Payne)

COLBERT, Général Auguste-François-Marie, Baron de Colbert de Chabanais (1779–1809)

The youngest of three sons of the Comte de Colbert-Chabanais, all of whom became cavalry generals in Napoleon's army, Auguste de Colbert achieved fame as one of his best light cavalry commanders (**see Plate J**). From the National Guard he rose through the ranks to gain a commission in 1795; served as ADC to Grouchy and Murat; was twice wounded at Acre, and was Murat's aide at Marengo. Promoted to command the 10e Chasseurs à Cheval, he served under Ney in 1805 and as *général de brigade* from that December, commanding the light cavalry brigade of Ney's VI Corps with distinction, notably at Jena. Ney paid testimony to his great abilities by remarking that he always slept peacefully when he knew that Colbert was commanding his outposts. In the Peninsula he led Ney's cavalry in the pursuit of Moore, and on 3 January 1809 led his brigade (3e Hussards and 15e Chasseurs) against

Moore's rearguard at Cacabellos. His success in driving back the British picquets may have led him to act imprudently, charging after the British over the bridge across the river Cua. They rode into a heavy crossfire; as one British observer remarked, 'I never saw men ride more handsomely to destruction', as 'we poured it into them right and left, and they went down like clockwork'[14]. It was said that one of the British commanders – perhaps Sir Edward Paget, though the point was later disputed – offered a cash prize to any man who brought down the gallant French officer on the grey horse. Whatever the case, a noted marksman, Thomas Plunket of the 95th Rifles, calmly took aim and shot Colbert through the head. Louis Lejeune wrote that his death was 'deeply regretted', for Colbert was 'a very interesting man, one of the flower of the army on account of his fine figure, his courteous bearing, and his chivalrous courage'[15]. Even the British were saddened; as Charles Steevens recalled, 'all of us who witnessed it, were very sorry, as he seemed to be a remarkably gallant fellow; but such, alas!, is the fate of war'[16].

CUSTINE DE SARRECK, Général Adam-Philippe, Comte de (1740–93)

One of the most unfortunate commanders of his era, Adam-Philippe Custine (**see Plate A**) was born at Metz, received his first nominal commission in the French army at the age of five years, and served in the Seven Years' War and in America, notably at Yorktown. *Maréchal de camp* from December 1781, he was elected to the States-General to represent the nobility of Metz; and as *lieutenant-général* from October 1791 he commanded the Army of the Vosges with some success, notably in the capture of Spire, Worms, Mainz and Frankfurt. Although a disciplinarian, he was popular with the army and was nicknamed (for an obvious reason) *'général moustache'*. After commanding the Armies of the Moselle and Rhine, in May 1793 he replaced Dampierre as commander of the Armies of the North and Ardennes, where he suffered reverses after initial success. These may have been the result of failings in military ability, but were insufficient to justify dismissal and arrest. Custine was tried on a number of curious charges, ranging from collaboration with the enemy to feeling pity for Louis XVI, for employing aristocratic officers and never entertaining Republicans at his table. Despite his protestations of innocence and the efforts of his daughter and his friends, he was condemned by the Revolutionary Tribunal and guillotined on 28 August 1793 – a most unjust end for one of the better French generals of the period.

The small central figure depicts General Adam-Philippe Custine, known as 'General Moustache' – see Plate A1 – accepting the surrender of Mainz (Mayence) from the Austrian governor Baron Gimnich on 21 October 1792. One of the better commanders of the early Revolutionary Wars, he was not permitted to extend his career: in 1793 those whom Sir Edward Cust described as 'his bloody masters' recalled him from the army, tried him on some very curious charges, and executed him. (Print after Victor Adam)

DAVOUT, Maréchal Louis-Nicolas, Duc d'Auerstädt, Prince d'Eckmühl (1770–1823)

Although not the most military in appearance of Napoleon's marshals, being bald and bespectacled, nevertheless Louis-Nicolas Davout (**see Plate D**) was probably the ablest and most formidable. From a noble family (the name was originally d'Avout) with a tradition of military service, he was commissioned into his father's cavalry regiment in 1788, but his support for revolutionary principles led to his dismissal. He re-entered military service as lieutenant-colonel of a volunteer battalion in 1791 and soon made his mark, if only by an unsuccessful attempt to apprehend the defecting Dumouriez. Although he became *général de brigade* in July 1793, he was forced to resign temporarily because of his aristocratic background, but was restored and served with distinction on the Rhine and in Egypt. *Général de division* from July 1800, he impressed Napoleon sufficiently to be the youngest of the first creation of the marshalate. Having divorced his first wife in 1794, he established a distant family connection with the Bonapartes by his marriage in 1801 to Aimee Leclerc, sister-in-law of Napoleon's sister Pauline.

Louis-Nicolas Davout, Duc d'Auerstädt, Prince d'Eckmühl – see Plate D2. Known initially as a cavalry leader, he had been commissioned originally into the Royal Champagne Regiment, in which his father had also served as an officer. Davout became perhaps the most able of all Napoleon's marshals; he was a noted disciplinarian and thus not always the most popular of commanders, but his commands always benefited from his careful superintendence. (Engraving by R.A.Muller after C.Gautherot)

Marshal Davout in full dress uniform, illustrating also the horse-furniture used by general officers – cf Plate I1. In addition to the usual distinctions of a marshal he wears the aiguillette of the Imperial Guard on his right shoulder, to which he was entitled by his appointment as *Colonel-Général* of the Grenadiers à Pied of the Guard. (Print by Lacoste & Moraine)

Though never very popular, a stern disciplinarian and without many gracious attributes, he was as concerned with the welfare of his men as with their training, and the formations he commanded were generally regarded as the best in the army, as appropriate for one nicknamed 'the Iron Marshal'. Personally courageous and with great abilities as a general, in 1805 he led III Corps in a famous forced march to Austerlitz. He won his greatest fame at Auerstädt in 1806, when he held at bay the larger part of the Prussian army while Napoleon crushed the remainder; he took the name of the battle as the title of the dukedom he received in 1808. Davout made the decisive flank-attack at Eylau and was further distinguished at Eckmuhl (for which he was awarded the title of prince in August of the same year, 1809) and at Wagram. In the Russian campaign of 1812 he led I Corps, which his careful command made the best in the army, and at Borodino recommended a wide flanking movement. This sensible proposal was rejected by Napoleon, who remarked that he was always for turning the enemy, but 'it is too dangerous a manoeuvre'[17], and the slaughter of a frontal attack ensued. Davout's battlefield skills were lost to Napoleon in 1813–14 when he was ordered to hold Hamburg; his stern governance there, as at Warsaw in 1807, led to further nicknames, 'Davout the Terrible' and 'the Hamburg Robespierre'.

Though he was a capable administrator, it is interesting to speculate on the outcome of the Hundred Days campaign had Davout been given a field command instead of the portfolios of minister of war and governor of Paris. After the final abdication he suffered two years of internal exile before he was reinstated by the Bourbons, and in 1819 became a member of the Chamber of Peers. Unswervingly loyal to Napoleon, devoted to his second wife (five of their eight children died in infancy or youth), and – unlike some marshals – not a plunderer, Davout had few equals as a fine commander who carried out his tasks with care, ability and resolution.

DESAIX DE VEYGOUX, Général Louis-Charles-Antoine (1768–1800)

One of the most popular and admired of French generals, Louis Desaix (**see Plate C**) was also one who helped to save Napoleon's reputation. A member of the impoverished nobility, he entered the French army as a subaltern in 1783 and, despite his background, supported the ideals of the Revolution. His abilities, and his refusal to emigrate like his family, brought swift promotion: a sub-lieutenant until November 1791, he was provisional *général de division* in October 1793, confirmed a year later. He won renown under Jourdan in 1795 and Moreau in 1796, notably in the defence of Kehl, but despite huge popularity he became a loyal subordinate of Napoleon. Originally commanding a division in the Egyptian campaign, while Napoleon was in Syria he conquered Upper Egypt with such humanity towards the

General Louis-Charles-Antoine Desaix – cf Plate C1. A number of early pictures show him wearing a plain civilian-style coat, and not all generals at this time wore the prescribed uniform. Barthélemy Joubert (1769–99), a general of great repute who was killed at Novi, recalled that at Loano he wore an ordinary soldier's coat and gaiters, so that he was not recognised when he called upon enemy officers to surrender. (Engraving by R.G.Tietze after J.B.P.Guérin)

23

The death of Desaix at Marengo: an early, though not wholly accurate depiction of the fall of the commander most responsible for saving Napoleon at this battle. As he began the vital advance at the head of the 9e Demi-Brigade Légère he fell dead from a shot through the heart, conceivably an accidental shot from his own side. Stories of a flamboyantly patriotic dying declaration are unconvincing, since the surgeons who embalmed his body were of the opinion that he must have been killed instantly. (Painting by J.F.J.Swebach-Desfontaines; the Royal Collection © 2000 HM Queen Elizabeth II)

civilian population that he was styled 'the Just Sultan'. He remained in Egypt after Napoleon returned to France, signing the Convention of El Arish, but on travelling back to France he was captured by the British.

As a general, Napoleon described him as 'well-squared' or well-balanced, in that courage and zeal were in equilibrium with thoughtful judgment; and his merits were proven at Marengo. Desaix had gained his freedom only just in time to take part in the battle, and having been detached from the main army he countermarched his troops towards the sound of gunfire. He arrived to find the French on the verge of defeat but, consulting his watch, remarked to Napoleon that although the battle was lost, there was yet time to win another. Napoleon recalled that he told Desaix that they should sit on the grass for a moment, to demonstrate their calmness to the soldiers; whereupon Desaix seemed to express a presentiment of death. If so, it was accurate: as he led the counter-attack which helped win the battle he was shot dead through the heart. Stories that he exclaimed to his aide, Anne-Charles Lebrun (son of the Third Consul), that he died with regret, 'because I feel that I have not done enough to be remembered by posterity'[18] are probably apocryphal, since the wound would have caused instantaneous death. His fall was lamented even by his enemies: the British *Monthly Review*, for example, stated that he had been esteemed by the French, 'honoured by the Austrians, and loved by all who knew him'[19]. Napoleon described his death as the greatest loss, for, he said, Desaix would never have been a rival, only a loyal colleague, who 'lived only for noble ambition and true glory; his character was formed on the ancient model'[20].

DORSENNE, Général Jean-Marie-Pierre-François Lepaige, Comte (1773–1812)

'*Le beau Dorsenne*' – 'handsome Dorsenne' – was one of the most famous officers of the Imperial Guard **(see Plate D)**. Enlisting as a volunteer in 1791, he was a captain by September 1792, and served with distinction in the Armies of the North and Sambre & Meuse before he attracted Napoleon's attention in Italy. Advanced to *chef de brigade* in Egypt, he joined the Grenadiers à Pied of the Imperial Guard in March 1805, rising to *général de brigade* after Austerlitz; he distinguished himself at Eylau and in 1808 became colonel of the Grenadiers. Dorsenne was the strictest of commandants: his weekly inspections of his guardsmen were, according the Jean-Roch Coignet, occasions to fear, with punishments handed out to those who exhibited even a speck of dirt as Dorsenne inspected fingernails and lifted up waistcoats to look at the shirts underneath. The maintenance of such discipline was repaid on the battlefield, however: at Essling the Guard stood immobile under fire, with Dorsenne setting the example while commanding the brigade of the Chasseurs and Grenadiers à Pied. Two horses were killed beneath him, so he stood on foot at the head of his men, covered in mud, and declared, 'Your general is not hurt. You may depend upon him, he will know how to die at his post'. As Coignet remarked, 'how grateful the country ought to be for such men!'[21]. Dorsenne was wounded in the head on that occasion, but survived. He was promoted to *général de division* in June 1809, serving at Wagram; commanded the Guard in Spain in the following year; and subsequently led the Army of the North in the Peninsula, numerically a larger command than that of any of the four marshals serving in Spain at that time. He relinquished this position in May 1812, and died in the following July, after a trepanning operation made necessary by his Essling wound.

DUMAS, Général Thomas-Alexandre – known as Davy de la Pailleterie (1762–1806)

Thomas-Alexandre Dumas **(see Plate B)** was one of the most distinguished of the French officers from San Domingo (Haiti), who included the great and tragic Toussaint L'Ouverture. Dumas was the illegitimate son of Antoine-Alexandre Davy, Marquis de la Pailleterie, and a local woman, Marie Cessette Dumas. In 1780 he accompanied his father to France and in 1786 enlisted as an ordinary dragoon. Commissioned a lieutenant in September 1792, he rose to *général de division* within a year; he commanded in the western Pyrenees and the Alps, led a cavalry division in the Army of Italy, and was cavalry commander in the Egyptian expedition. He was clearly a remarkable individual, and his physical strength was also legendary: it was said that he could lift four muskets by inserting his fingers into the barrels. For holding a bridge single-handed he was nicknamed 'the Horatius of the Tyrol' (after the Roman hero Horatius Cocles, who according to tradition defended the Sublician Bridge across the Tiber to save Rome), and another nickname from his Tyrolean campaigning was 'the Black Devil'. He acted as spokesman for those generals who were critical of the Egyptian campaign and Napoleon's conduct of it, so that when he requested leave on the grounds that the climate was damaging his health Napoleon let him go willingly; this ended his active military

Commemorating a fallen hero: an unsigned copper medallion struck to perpetuate the memory of Desaix. The reverse inscription records his service at Kehl and in Upper Egypt and his death at Marengo, a victory 'bought with his blood'. It describes him as *'brave'* and *'juste'*, an assessment apparently universal at the time.

career. His son and grandson achieved perhaps greater fame than the descendants of any other French general of the period: they were the authors Alexandre Dumas father (1802–70) and son (1824–95).

DUROC, Général Géraud-Christophe-Michel, Duc de Frioul (1772–1813)

Perhaps Napoleon's best and most trusted friend, Duroc **(see Plate F)** was the son of a French officer and began his military training before the Revolution. After a brief emigration, he was commissioned in the artillery in June 1793; he met Napoleon at Toulon, and served as his aide in Italy and Egypt, sustaining a severe wound at Aboukir. Although he became *général de brigade* (1801) and *de division* (1803), he became much more than just Napoleon's senior ADC, being entrusted with important diplomatic missions; these included the negotiations of the Treaty of Schönbrunn and for the abdication of Charles IV of Spain. Appointed as Napoleon's Grand Marshal of the Palace (1805) and ennobled as Duke of Friuli in May 1808, he led Oudinot's grenadiers at Austerlitz, but in most campaigns was usually at Napoleon's side as the very capable director of the imperial household.

The death of Duroc at Bautzen, 1813; Napoleon weeps for his stricken friend. Conscious, and knowing that his wound was mortal, Duroc asked only for opium to dull the pain. Napoleon was so affected that he could not bear to remain long, but went away and walked up and down in an attempt to compose himself; when someone asked him for orders he replied, 'Ask me nothing until tomorrow'. (Engraving after Horace Vernet)

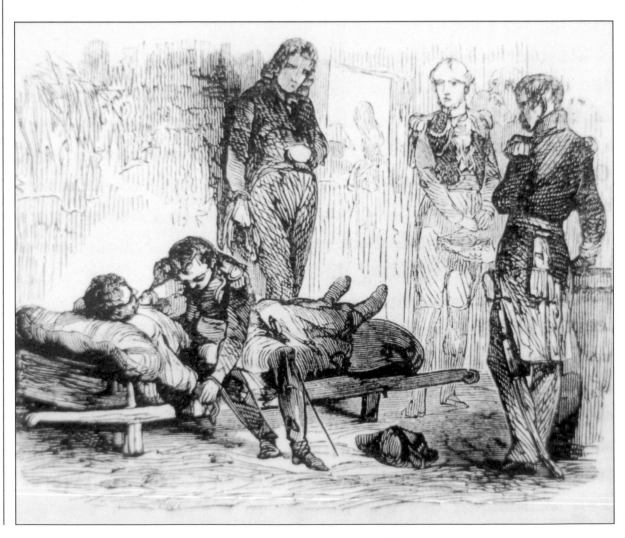

Napoleon remarked to Las Cases that Duroc was the only individual who possessed his entire confidence, and despite what appeared to be a cold manner, 'he was a pure and virtuous man, utterly disinterested, and extremely generous'. As an adviser he was invaluable to Napoleon, and was said to know him so well that he would fail to execute orders issued in a temper: 'How many storms has he soothed! how many rash orders, given in the moment of irritation, has he omitted to execute, knowing that his master would thank him next day for the omission! The Emperor had accommodated himself to this sort of tacit agreement; and on that account gave way the more readily to those violent bursts of temper, which relieve by the vent they afford to the passions'[22].

It was thus a great tragedy for Napoleon when, at Bautzen in 1813, Duroc was struck in the lower abdomen by the same ball which killed the engineer general François-Joseph Kirgener. The wound was mortal, but Duroc lived long enough for an interview with Napoleon which was described as heartbreaking, and which the emperor left in tears and entirely distracted – even in later years the recollection caused him anguish. He was so affected by Duroc's death that when he was again in the area some three months later Napoleon took care to show Murat the spot where he had been hit, and gave a substantial sum to the farmer on whose land he had died for the erection of a monument in his memory. As Las Cases commented, Duroc was one of those whose value is only truly appreciated after his death, adding that the loss to Napoleon of so wise and trusted an adviser was a 'national calamity'.

HAUTPOUL, Général Jean-Joseph Ange, Comte d' (1754–1807)

A member of an old aristocratic family, Hautpoul (see Plate G) enlisted in the French cavalry in 1771 and was commissioned in 1777; but his promotion was slow, and not until 1792 did he become a captain. His bearing and manner were not those which might have been expected of a nobleman; he spoke the language like a common soldier and his demeanour was bluff, one biographer comparing his 'rough-hewn grandeur' of appearance with that of a warrior from Renaissance art [23]. He served in the early Revolutionary Wars as a lieutenant-colonel, and such was his popularity with his men that an attempt to deprive him of rank on account of his noble ancestry was prevented when they threatened to mutiny. Provisionally a *général de brigade* in 1794 and *de division* in 1797, he served with distinction in the early campaigns and was wounded in the shoulder at Altenkirchen. Jourdan blamed the misbehaviour of his men for the defeat of Stockach, but Hautpoul was acquitted by court-martial and went on to serve with especial distinction at Hohenlinden. In 1805 he became particularly associated with the relatively newly-created arm of the Cuirassiers, and distinguished himself at the head of the 2nd Heavy Cavalry Division at Austerlitz.

He resigned his command on being appointed a senator, but was back for the war against Prussia, including Jena. In the 1807 campaign he made a devastating attack during the action at Hoff (6 February), in recognition of which Napoleon embraced him in view of his division. It was said that the embarrassed Hautpoul remarked that the only way to become worthy of such an honour was to get himself killed in Napoleon's service, and his words were terribly prophetic. Two days later he led his command in the great charges which helped save Napoleon at Eylau, but he was hit in the thigh by a grapeshot, which broke the bone. Two great medical experts were divided over treatment: Pierre-François Percy believed the leg could be saved, but Dominique-Jean Larrey recommended amputation to save his life. Hautpoul chose to keep the leg, but Larrey was right, and he died on 14 February, greatly lamented not only as a skilled commander of heavy cavalry but also for his human qualities.

HULIN, Général Pierre-Augustin, Comte (1758–1841)

Although not one of the most familiar of Napoleon's generals, Hulin (see Plate D) featured in two of the most important incidents of Napoleon's reign. A Parisian who enrolled in the French army as a private soldier in 1771, his service was unremarkable until the Revolution, when (having taken his discharge in 1787) he was one of the stormers of the Bastille. Resuming military service as an officer in 1789, he progressed from the National Guard to a variety of staff appointments, meanwhile surviving almost a year in prison (1793–94). He was appointed commandant of the Grenadiers à Pied of the Consular Guard in September 1802, and *général de brigade* in the following August. In 1804 he presided over the commission which tried and condemned the Duc d'Enghien, one of the crimes for which Napoleon was most criticised. After campaign service with the Guard, in August 1807 Hulin was promoted to *général de division* and appointed governor of Paris, an office which he held until 1814, and again during the Hundred Days. In this post he rendered his most important service to Napoleon, when he was one of the few officials to resist the mad *coup d'état* of Général Claude-François de Malet while Napoleon was preoccupied in Russia. Hulin was shot by Malet as he tried to arrest him, but following Hulin's resistance the conspirators were seized, condemned and shot; so that although Hulin was a relatively minor personality, Napoleon had good reason to be thankful for his courage. Upon the second Bourbon restoration Hulin was exiled, but permitted to return to France in 1819.

JUNOT, Général Jean-Andoche, Duc d'Abrantes (1771–1813)

One of Napoleon's most colourful subordinates, Junot (see Plate E) was a law student at the beginning of the Revolution. He joined a volunteer battalion; was twice wounded; and owed his first advancement to an incident at Toulon when, as a sergeant, his cool courage under fire while taking dictation from Napoleon impressed the young officer. He served as Napoleon's ADC in Italy, receiving a head wound at Lonato which may have contributed to his later mental problems. *Général de brigade* from January 1799, he survived the Egyptian campaign but was wounded in a duel and was captured by the British as he tried to return

Jean-Andoche Junot, Duc d'Abrantes. This portrait of the flamboyant general shows a version of the uniform of *Colonel-Général* of Hussars, similar to that depicted in Plate E1 but with some minor variations, including the wearing of a very elaborate pouch-belt and collar (and presumably cuffs) edged with broad gold lace rather than the gold oak-leaf embroidery of a general. (Engraving by T.Read)

Junot first impressed Napoleon with his calmness under fire when both were serving at Toulon, Napoleon as artillery commander and Junot as an enlisted man. Deputed to take Napoleon's dictation because of his ability to read and write, Sergeant Junot was writing when the near impact of a roundshot threw earth all over them both. Unshaken by his close escape, Junot merely remarked that he would not now need sand to blot his ink. (Engraving after Horace Vernet)

home. On that return, he was appointed commandant of Paris and *général de division* (November 1801).

In October 1800 he had married Laure-Adélaide-Constance Permon (1783–1834), a woman noted for beauty and wit, but also for great extravagance – a failing shared by Junot, who was constantly in financial difficulties compounded by his dissipated lifestyle. Napoleon complained that the amount of money he gave Junot 'almost exceeded belief, and yet he was always in debt'. When he tried to teach Laure how to manage her finances, 'she grew angry and treated me like a child; nothing then remained for me to do but send her about her business, and abandon her to her fate'[24].

After serving as ambassador to Portugal and as Napoleon's aide in the 1805 campaign, as governor of Parma and Piacenza and of Paris, Junot led the invasion of Portugal in 1807. Early success was rewarded with the dukedom of Abrantes, though Junot greatly resented not having been appointed as a marshal; and it was followed by defeat at Vimeiro. In 1809 he commanded at the siege of Saragossa, and only with difficulty was persuaded to countermand the order for a suicidal assault in order to gain the credit for himself before he was superseded by Lannes; Lejeune thought that 'his readily aroused jealousy and excessive arrogance were really the first symptoms of a mental malady which was beginning to get a hold on him'[25]. After commanding the reserve army in Germany in 1809 Junot returned to the Peninsula, serving at Busaco and Fuentes de Oñoro. In the Russian campaign of 1812 he was originally deputy to Eugène de Beauharnais with IV Corps, until in late July he replaced Jérôme Bonaparte as commander of VIII Corps. He was not a success, being criticised over the escape of Barclay as he withdrew from Smolensk; Napoleon remarked that Junot no longer appeared to be the same man, and committed great errors. As a consequence he was recalled to France in January 1813 and given the relatively unimportant posts of governor of Venice, and later governor-general of Illyria. As his mental problems intensified he had to be relieved of duty; taken to his father's house at Montbard, he died on 29 July 1813 as a consequence of leaping from a window in his derangement, and finally of 'having mutilated his person with his own hands'[26] – a sad end for one of Napoleon's most flamboyant, if troublesome subordinates.

KELLERMANN, Maréchal François-Christophe, Duc de Valmy (1735–1820)

As his name suggests, François Kellermann (see Plate A) was a member of a Saxon family long settled in Strasbourg, who spoke French with a strong accent and began his career as a volunteer in a German regiment in French service in 1752. Commissioned in the following year, his progress through the ranks was not rapid but based entirely upon his own abilities, his middle-class background offering none of the advantages conferred by being a member of the nobility. Described – accurately – as an intelligent, good officer, he achieved the rank of general by 1784 and became *lieutenant-général* in March 1792. An able administrator, when he succeeded Luckner in command of the Army of the Centre in August 1792 he rapidly improved its organisation and combat capability. Ordered to assist Dumouriez in the following month, it was Kellermann's army which halted the enemy at Valmy, although this decisive action can hardly be accorded the status of a battle: Kellermann's artillery delivered so effective a bombardment that the Prussians were discouraged from pressing home their attack, and casualties were light on both sides. Nevertheless, Kellermann's personal contribution was decisive: his presence heartened his men and prevented panic after several caissons blew up. Most of his troops were regulars, and it is somewhat ironic that the new Republic was saved by the old Royal army, commanded by a general of Royalist origin.

Although hailed as the saviour of the Revolution, that very background raised political suspicions, and he was suspended and imprisoned for some thirteen months. Upon acquittal his rank was restored, and in March 1795 he was given command of the Armies of the Alps and Italy, restricted to command of the former from September; and his front-line career ended with the disbandment of that army in September 1797, without the opportunity

François-Christophe Kellermann, Duc de Valmy, in the uniform of a marshal. Although his front line service ended in 1797 he remained valuable to Napoleon throughout the period in a series of administrative or second line commands; as late as 1813 he was leading the 'Corps of Observation of the Rhine' in his 78th year. In this portrait the second breast star, below that of the Légion d'Honneur, is presumably that of the Golden Eagle of Württemberg, which he was awarded in 1806.

of serving in a major campaign. He did not retire, however; he entered politics as a senator from December 1799, and although his elevation to the marshalate – he was the oldest member of the original creation in 1804 – was largely honorary, as was his dukedom of Valmy (1808), his organisational ability continued to prove extremely useful to Napoleon as commander of a number of reserve formations, and even at the age of 79 he remained a valuable asset.

Having served under Royal, Republican and Imperial regimes he survived the Bourbon restoration with reputation intact, as deserved by his years of hard and productive effort. His son, the cavalry general François-Etienne Kellermann, was perhaps the better-known of the two.

KLÉBER, Général Jean-Baptiste (1753–1800)

One of the most famous generals of the Revolutionary period, Kléber (see Plate B) was the son of a mason, born at Strasbourg and trained as an architect. After instruction at the Bavarian military school he was commissioned in the Austrian army, but since he did not see much hope of promotion he resigned and became inspector of public buildings at Belfort. He joined the National Guard in 1789 and at the beginning of the Revolutionary Wars was elected to field rank. He became *général de brigade* in August 1793 after service at Mainz, and *de division* in October 1793 following service against the Vendée rebels. Recalled for advocating leniency towards them, Kléber subsequently served with distinction with the Army of the Sambre & Meuse, at Fleurus and at Neuweid in October 1795. Though he commanded an army several times on a provisional basis, he was dissatisfied with the recognition he received and resigned in December 1796. He returned to the service as a divisional commander in Napoleon's expedition to Egypt; a head wound at Alexandria prevented further battlefield service until the Syrian campaign of 1799, when he led his division with distinction, notably at Mount Tabor.

He was not enthusiastic about the expedition and evidently came to hate Napoleon for his ambition, making jokes and cartoons about him; and though Napoleon appointed him to command the army when he himself went home, this appointment was perhaps intended to keep a source of potential discontent out of the way. Kléber felt himself abandoned, and his situation was certainly perilous, so he concluded the Convention of El Arish with Sidney Smith. Nevertheless, when this was not ratified he took the offensive, and his victory at Heliopolis (20 March 1800) permitted the re-occupation of Cairo. On 14 June, however, as he was walking in his garden, he was stabbed to death by a fanatic, Suliman El-Halebi ('of Aleppo' – 1773–1800), who was subsequently captured and executed with extreme barbarity.

Despite appearing to lack self-belief, Kléber was as adept at administration as in battlefield command, and his death was a severe

Jean-Baptiste Kléber, who succeeded Napoleon in command of the French forces in Egypt, where he met his death – two of an assassin's four stab wounds pierced his heart. An imposing figure, tall and well-built, Kléber remarked to Napoleon while in the trenches before Acre that the trench might be deep enough to shelter Napoleon but that it barely covered half his taller frame. (Engraving by T.Johnson after Guérin) loss. Napoleon said that he was 'endowed with the highest talent [and] pursued glory as the only road to enjoyment; but he had no national sentiment, and he could, without any sacrifice, have devoted himself to foreign service'. He added, however, that Kléber and Desaix had been his best lieutenants, Desaix's talents the result of education and experience, Kléber's those of nature: 'The genius of Kléber only burst forth at particular moments, when roused by the importance of the occasion; and then it immediately slumbered again in the bosom of indolence and pleasure'[(27)]. Remarkably, both Desaix and Kléber were killed on the same day.

LANNES, Maréchal Jean, Duc de Montebello (1769–1809)

Napoleon once remarked that Jean Lannes (**see Plate L**) was his best friend; some would say that truly disinterested friendship was probably not in Bonaparte's character, but certainly none was a braver or more loyal friend toward him than Lannes. The son of a farmer and livery stable keeper at Lectoure, and apprenticed to a dyer, Lannes had little education but became an officer shortly after his enlistment in 1792. His military talents were obvious, and in Italy Napoleon promoted him to *général de brigade* provisionally in September 1796. Wounded several times (three times at Arcola alone), he became a staunch friend of Napoleon, and was appointed *général de division* in May 1799, two days after being shot in the neck at Acre, a wound from which he never fully recovered – thereafter his head was inclined slightly to the left, and he suffered pain in his throat. Further distress at this time was caused by his divorce, upon learning that his wife, whom he had not seen for two years, had had a child. Lannes accompanied Napoleon from Egypt and assisted in the *coup* of Brumaire. He was appointed to command the Consular Guard, but left them after spending upon them money not authorised, which he had to pay back in person thanks to a loan from Augereau. In the 1800 campaign he commanded the advance guard of the Army of Reserve; won the battle of Montebello (from where the title of his dukedom was taken when it was bestowed in 1808); and played an important part in the victory of Marengo.

Jean Lannes, one of Napoleon's closest friends, in an early portrait as a regimental officer (his first commission was in the 2nd Gers Bn in 1792). His rise through the ranks was rapid, despite his having received only limited education; he was taught to read and write by one of his brothers, a priest. (Engraving by Kruell after Guérin)

He was less successful as ambassador to Portugal, being unsuited to diplomacy, and his conduct there led to a hostile British description of him as 'one of those insolent upstarts that sprouted from the feculence of the French Revolution [who] carried his deportment to a pitch of arrogance and outrage unexampled in the History of Diplomacy'! [(28)].

Created a marshal in 1804, Lannes commanded V Corps in the Austerlitz campaign and in 1806, when he won the action at Saalfeld and was distinguished at Jena; though wounded at Pultusk, he fought at Heilsberg and Friedland. His ADC Marbot described him as usually calm and placid, but one who could fly into a rage on the battlefield if his orders were not performed correctly. After hearing Napoleon say that he would never be a great general unless he could control his temper,

(continued on page 45)

1: Général Adam-Philippe Custine, c1792
2: Général Napoleon Bonaparte, c1796
3: Général François-Christophe Kellermann, c1796

A

1: Général Thomas-Alexandre Dumas (a.k.a. Davy de la Pailleterie)
2: Officer, Bonaparte's Guides (Nicolas Dahlmann)
3: Général Jean-Baptiste Kléber

1: Général Louis-Charles-Antoine Desaix
2: ADC to Général de Division
3: Napoleon Bonaparte, 1800

P. Courcelle

C

1: Général J.M.P.F.L. Dorsenne
2: Maréchal Louis-Nicolas Davout
3: Général Pierre-Augustin Hulin

D

1: Général Jean-Andoche Junot
2: Louis Bonaparte, King of Holland
3: Maréchal André Massena

E

F

1: Général Géraud-Christophe-Michel Duroc,
  as Grand Marshal of the Palace
2: Maréchal Claude Victor (Perrin)
3: Maréchal Charles-Pierre-François Augereau

1: Général Jean-Joseph Ange, Comte d'Hautpoul
2: Général Antoine-Charles-Louis Lasalle
3: Colonel-Major Louis Lepic

G

1: Joseph-François Bernadotte
2: Maréchal Jean-Baptiste-Jules Bernadotte
3: ADC to Bernadotte

H

1: Maréchal A.E.C.J. Mortier
2: Trooper, Mortier's Guides
3: Trooper, Bernadotte's Guides

P. Courcelle

1: Maréchal Jean-Baptiste Bessières
2: Général Auguste-François-Marie de Colbert
3: Général Charles Lefebvre-Desnouettes

P. Courcelle

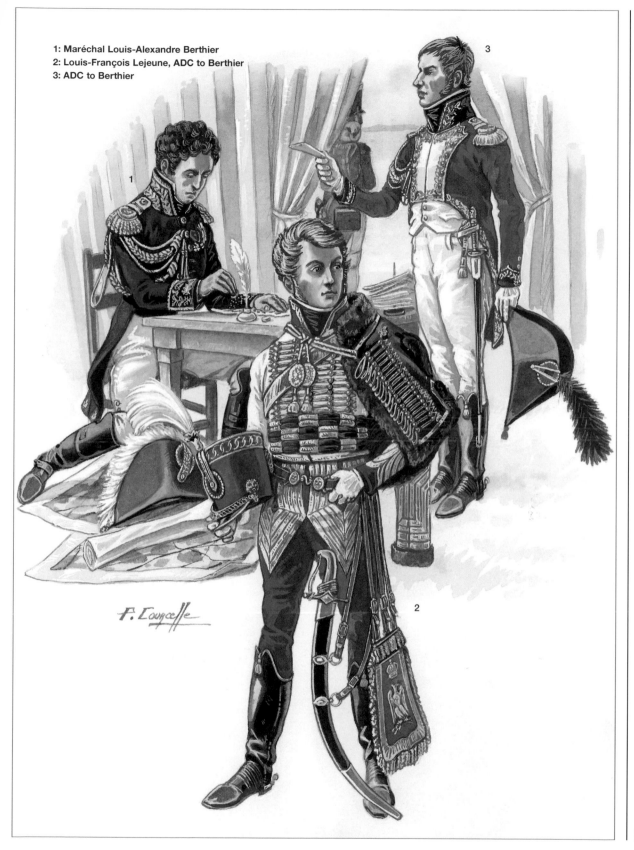

1: Maréchal Louis-Alexandre Berthier
2: Louis-François Lejeune, ADC to Berthier
3: ADC to Berthier

F. Courcelle

K

1: Général de Brigade
2: Maréchal Jean Lannes
3: Colonel of Engineers (Guillaume Dode)

P. Courcelle

L

Lannes tried to keep his emotions in check, turning pale and clenching his fists in an attempt to prevent an outburst. He went to Spain with Napoleon, won the battle of Tudela and successfully concluded the siege of Saragossa, before returning to Germany to lead a corps at Abensberg, Eckmühl and Ratisbon. At the storming of the latter he horrified his staff by threatening to be first up a scaling-ladder.

Leading the new II Corps at Aspern-Essling, he was ordered to hold the latter village. When his old friend Général Pierre Pouzet (1766–1809) was killed at his side, Lannes was sitting on a bank to recover from the shock when a roundshot smashed one knee and damaged the other. As he was carried away Napoleon flung himself upon the litter, reducing to tears all who witnessed the scene. Larrey amputated one leg and it seemed as if Lannes might recover, but septicaemia set in and he died on 31 May 1809. Napoleon was desolated

Leading from the front – a marshal sets the example. At the storm of Ratisbon on 23 April 1809 Lannes grew angry with the hesitation of his troops to rush the breach under murderous fire. Declaring that he was a grenadier before he was a marshal, and was a grenadier still, he seized a scaling-ladder and would have led the attack in person had his aides not dragged the ladder from him and led the assault themselves, followed by the troops who had been encouraged by their marshal's bravery. (Print after A.Paris)

by grief, sitting in tears by the body until Berthier dragged him away; he realised that he had lost not only a skilled and fearless general but also perhaps his only true friend. 'I was for him something vague and undefined, a superior being', commented Napoleon, while 'he was assuredly one of the men on whom I could most implicitly rely. It is very true that, in the impetuosity of his disposition, he has sometimes suffered some hasty expressions against me to escape his lips, but he would probably have broken the head of any person who had chanced to hear them'. He also wrote that while in Lannes courage at first predominated over judgment, the latter was increasing so that he had become a very capable commander: 'I found him a dwarf, but I lost him a giant'[29].

LASALLE, Général Antoine-Charles-Louis, Comte (1775–1809)

Général Maximilien Foy considered that Napoleon's army boasted only four cavalry commanders of the greatest skill: Murat, Kellermann, Montbrun and Lasalle **(see Plate G)**, and few would have disputed his choice of the latter. Born at Metz into a noble family, Lasalle was commissioned in the French army in 1786, and having been deprived of his rank by the Revolution re-enlisted as a private soldier. Almost ten years elapsed between his second commission and his promotion to *général de brigade* (1805), but his reputation grew steadily from an early stage of his career. In some respects he was a strange contradiction: one of the best commanders of light cavalry, he was extremely talented both on the battlefield and in outpost duty, was handsome, intelligent, well-educated and witty; yet, according to Marbot, he posed as a ruffian who 'might always be seen drinking, swearing, and smashing everything'[30]. In this he was regarded as the archetypal hussar, flamboyant and fearless, with a cultivated swagger – an attitude epitomised by his remark that any hussar who was not dead by the age of thirty was a blackguard.

Lasalle served at Austerlitz, but his greatest triumph was at Stettin in October 1806, which city he deceived into capitulation despite having only a small force of cavalry at his disposal. Promoted to *général de division* the following December, he further distinguished himself in Spain, notably at Medina del Rio Seco and Medellin. Lasalle was popular not only with the army but also with Napoleon, who excused his behaviour off the battlefield and his squandering of money. On one occasion, when Lasalle was reported by a prefect for rowdy conduct, Napoleon issued only a mild reprimand and remarked that although it

Antoine-Charles-Louis Lasalle, the archetypal hussar. For all the swaggering and boastful manner which Lasalle cultivated, he was the ultimate professional as a leader of light cavalry. His brigade – the 5e and 7e Hussars – performed prodigies in the pursuit of the Prussians after Jena in 1806, his lightning advance culminating in the capture, by bluff, of some 6,000 men and 120 guns at Stettin, by about 700 French troopers. His career was as colourful as the image he presented; at Heilsberg, for instance, he and Murat saved each other's lives. (Engraving by Forestier after Gros)

Lasalle as *général de division*, a rank he attained in December 1806 – cf Plate G2. Here the three silver stars indicative of this rank are displayed on the knot of the tasselled end of the sash, and upon the raquettes which fasten the neck of his pelisse, worn here over a braided waistcoat. Note the two characteristic items associated with Lasalle: the loose, false-booted overalls which came to bear his name, and the large pipe. (Print after François Flameng)

took only the stroke of a pen to create a prefect, it took twenty years to make a Lasalle. Recalled from Spain, in the 1809 Danube campaign Lasalle led the 1st Light Cavalry Division at Aspern-Essling, but while leading his troops at Wagram he was shot through the head and killed. Marbot remarked that Lasalle had not provided the best model for emulation, in that one who tried to imitate him could become another 'reckless, drinking, swearing rowdy', but without possessing the merits which permitted such conduct to be tolerated. Nonetheless, his death deprived Napoleon of one of the best and most professional of his cavalry commanders, and certainly one of the most colourful.

LEFEBVRE-DESNOUETTES, Général Charles, Comte (1773–1822)

One of Napoleon's favourites, Charles Lefebvre-Desnouettes **(see Plate J)** was born in Paris, the son of a draper, who three times ran away to the army (his parents buying his discharge each time) until he achieved his ambition of a military career. After a short time in the ranks he was commissioned in the 5e Dragons in February 1793, and after wide service came to Napoleon's notice, serving as his ADC in the Marengo campaign. After service at Elchingen and Austerlitz with the cavalry, he became *général de brigade* in September 1806. In 1806–07 he served as ADC, later grand equerry, to Jérôme Bonaparte, and was a *général de division* in Westphalian service. He was promoted to that rank in the French army after his return to French service in 1808, and became colonel-major of the Chasseurs à Cheval of the Imperial Guard. Ennobled as a count in March 1808, he not only commanded Napoleon's favourite regiment, but was even allied to the imperial family by his marriage to Napoleon's second cousin.

He went to Spain as Bessières' chief of staff, was wounded at Saragossa (the siege of which he began), and returned to the Peninsula later in the same year (1808) in command of his Guard Chasseurs. Leading them in the pursuit of Moore's army, on 29 December he came up with the British rearguard at Benavente. Although under orders not to hazard his regiment, he led them across the river Esla, only to be driven back by a vigorous British counter-attack; with his horse wounded, he was captured by Private Levi Grisdale of the British 10th Hussars. (At least, Grisdale claimed the credit, though apparently Private Johan Bergmann of the King's German Legion was also involved; but being 'an extremely simple fellow' the latter omitted to claim his share in the capture [31]). It was reported that Napoleon was notably displeased at Lefebvre-Desnouettes' recklessness.

He was taken to England and lived at Cheltenham on parole, until with the assistance of his wife he escaped to France in 1812. He led the Guard Chasseurs in Russia later that year, being wounded at Vinkovo; led the 1st Guard Cavalry Division in 1813, and in 1814 was twice bayoneted at Bayonne. At the Restoration he retained command of the ex-Guard Chasseurs, but helped facilitate Napoleon's return, and commanded the Guard Light Cavalry division at Waterloo. His unswerving loyalty to Napoleon led to his proscription at the Second Restoration, and he fled to America under sentence of death. Offered a pardon, he sailed for Europe in 1822, but on 22 April of that year the ship in which he was travelling foundered off the coast of Ireland with the loss of all aboard.

The courtesies of a bygone age are recalled by the anecdote that following his capture at Benavente his baggage and servants were permitted to join him under a flag of truce so that he could appear smartly dressed when he dined with General Moore that evening; and when he appeared embarrassed at not having his sword (which had been

Charles Lefebvre-Desnouettes wearing the uniform of a general officer. The breast stars are those of the Orders of Fidelity of Baden, and of Military Merit of Maximilian Joseph of Bavaria. One of Napoleon's most favoured generals, he somewhat damaged his reputation by breaking his parole to escape from captivity in England. This was not only a personally dishonourable act by the standards of the day, but might have cast into doubt the future availability of parole for other captured officers.

lost in the fight), Moore removed his own so as to put the captive at ease. Such behaviour reflects as much upon Moore, of course, as upon the regard in which Lefebvre-Desnouettes was held by his enemies.

LEPIC, Général Louis, Comte (1765–1827)

Although not among the best-known of Napoleon's commanders, Louis Lepic (see Plate G) was one of the personalities of the Imperial Guard, and most remembered for one remarkable action. Joining the French cavalry as a private soldier in 1781, he was a corporal in Louis XVI's Constitutional Guard and was commissioned in 1792. After a number of campaigns and several wounds, in 1805 he was appointed colonel-major of the Grenadiers à Cheval of the Imperial Guard, one of the most prestigious regiments of the army. His greatest fame came at Eylau, where he led his regiment despite suffering from severe rheumatism. It was as they sat immobile under heavy artillery fire that Lepic called out his famous remark: 'Heads up! Those are bullets, not turds!' – an incident immortalised by Detaille's painting of the incident, entitled by the French version of his exclamation: *'Haut les têtes! Le mitraille n'est pas de la merde!'* More significant, however, was Lepic's leadership in the great cavalry charges which followed. He took his men through the Russian lines, rallied, and, declining a call to surrender, fought his way back, wounded. Napoleon remarked that his arrival was so late that he feared him captured, whereupon Lepic answered that the only report Napoleon would ever receive would be of his death, never of his capture. He subsequently served at Wagram.

Appointed *général de brigade*, he served with the Guard cavalry in the Peninsula, and in 1811 at Fuentes de Oñoro he led a brigade including not only members of his own regiment but Chasseurs, Lancers and Mamelukes as well. When in this action he was ordered to charge, he replied that he had orders to move only with Bessières' express permission, and Marbot recorded that he was biting his sword-blade with frustration at this enforced inactivity. After service in Russia in 1812 Lepic became *général de division* in February 1813, and colonel of the 2e Gardes d'Honneur of the Imperial Guard later in the same year. He had no further military employment following the Hundred Days.

MASSENA, Maréchal André, Duc de Rivoli, Prince d'Essling (1758–1817)

One of the oldest of Napoleon's comrades, André Massena (see Plate E) was a native of Nice, at that time part of Piedmont, and so was Italian by birth; indeed, his name was sometimes spelled 'Andrea'. The son of a small businessman, he was orphaned and raised by an uncle, but having no enthusiasm for the latter's soap-making business he went to sea as a cabin boy. When that failed to suit him he joined the French army in 1775, but left (as a sergeant-major) in 1789 to become a fruit-merchant and smuggler. After joining the Antibes National Guard, however, his

André Massena, wearing the uniform of a general prior to his appointment as marshal. Although his name is often associated with his command of the Army of Portugal, and he was certainly a formidable opponent of Wellington in the Peninsula, his greatest successes were achieved at an earlier period, notably when in independent command in Switzerland in 1799.

promotion was rapid: *général de brigade* in August 1793, *de division* in December. The talents which led to this swift rise in rank were demonstrated with the Army of Italy, where Napoleon described him as active, tireless and quick-witted. He was greatly distinguished at Rivoli (from where the title of his dukedom was taken in 1808), and it was there that Napoleon described him as 'dear child of victory' – though the word he actually used was 'spoilt', not 'dear'.

According to Napoleon, Massena's military skill was instinctive, his lack of education leading him not to know what he intended to do before he entered a field of battle; but once there the necessary balance between courage and judgment was 'created in the midst of danger', and he seemed to know intuitively what to do. Furthermore, Napoleon commented, he was 'endowed with extraordinary courage and firmness, which seemed to increase in excess of danger. When conquered, he was always ready to fight the battle again as though he had been the conqueror'[32]. Marbot, who knew him well, also described him as a 'born general', though one without cultivation or candour and with tendencies towards bearing malice and avarice. The latter was certainly true: Massena was a noted plunderer and acquirer of wealth by dubious means.

Of his military skill there was no doubt: in 1798 his greatest victory was at the second Battle of Zurich when commanding the Army of Switzerland, though while leading the Army of Italy in 1800 he was besieged in Genoa and compelled by starvation to surrender. Among the first creation of the marshalate, in 1805 he led the Army of Italy and in 1807, V Corps. Having lost an eye in a shooting accident in 1808 (Napoleon was the culprit but faithful Berthier took the blame), he led IV Corps in the war against Austria. At Aspern-Essling he performed heroically in covering the army's retreat; Lejeune wrote of his inspirational leadership, as he stood unmoved while shot smashed the trees around him, 'calmly indifferent to the fall of the branches brought down upon his head by the showers of grape-shot and bullets... his look and voice, stern as the *quos ego* of Virgil's angry Neptune, inspiring all who surrounded him with irresistible strength'[33]. It was from this action that Massena took the title of prince, awarded in January 1810. Later in this campaign he had to command from his carriage following a fall from his horse, and when appointed to command the Army of Portugal in April 1810 he was perhaps past his best; Marbot remarked that as he grew older, 'he pushed caution to the point of timidity, in fear of compromising the reputation he had earned'[34].

Although suffering from opposition and ill-will among his senior commanders, and distracted by his mistress Mme Leberton (who accompanied the headquarters on campaign), Massena was judged by Wellington to be 'the ablest after Napoleon'[35]; when ranged against him the duke had to be constantly on the alert, for 'I found him oftenest where I wished him not to be'[36]. Nevertheless, Massena was defeated at Busaco and Fuentes de Oñoro, and had to retreat from Portugal with great loss when confronted by the Lines of Torres Vedras. This led to his recall in April 1811, and Napoleon was distinctly uncharitable towards his old comrade. This effectively ended his career, though from April 1813 he commanded the Toulon military district. Massena's support for Napoleon during the Hundred Days was somewhat lukewarm, and though appointed to lead the Paris National Guard by the provisional

This portrait of Massena tends to confirm Marbot's description of his physical appearance as lean and spare and of rather less than average height; he also remarked that Massena had 'a highly expressive Italian face'.
(Engraving by G.Dorrington after M.Jacque)

government after Waterloo he was replaced by the Bourbons. Nevertheless, despite this late eclipse, and his bad reputation for looting and lechery, his standing as one of the leading commanders of the era was fully justified.

MOREAU, Général Jean-Victor-Marie (1763–1813)

A general of considerable skill, Jean Moreau was for a time a rival to Napoleon, which led to his demise. A native of Morlaix in Brittany (east of Brest in the Finistère region), he was destined to follow his father's legal profession, but it was not to his taste. When he first ran away to the army he was bought out by his father; but later, having been a leader of the students while studying at Rennes, he became an officer in the town's National Guard. After service in the early campaigns as a field officer, his talents were recognised, notably by Carnot, and he became provisional *général de brigade* in December 1793, *de division* in April 1794. He succeeded Pichegru in command of the Armies of the North and of the Rhine & Moselle, and achieved some success, even conducting his retreat with distinction. He retained a devotion to his country even after his father, known in Morlaix as 'the father of the poor', was guillotined during the Terror.

Delays in revealing what he had discovered about Pichegru's correspondence with the enemy led to his dismissal from command, but his talents could not be ignored; in April 1799 he was given command of the Army of Italy, and then removed to the Army of the Rhine. He remained in Italy temporarily to serve under his successor, Barthelémy Joubert, and resumed command after the latter was killed at Novi. Greatly dissatisfied with the Directory, he assisted Napoleon in the *coup* of Brumaire and, leading his Army of the Rhine, won his great victory at Hohenlinden (3 December 1800) which, with Marengo, settled the war.

At this stage Moreau rivalled Napoleon in popularity, though not so complete a general. Napoleon thought that 'in him nature had left her work unfinished; he possessed more instinct than genius... destitute of invention [and] not sufficiently decided'[37], and so cautious as to be best-suited for a defensive role. Las Cases recorded a similar opinion expressed by Moreau's friend Général Jean-Maximilien Lamarque, who said that if he and Napoleon had opposed each other on the battlefield he would have favoured Moreau's troops, 'which were sure to be managed with the utmost regularity, precision, and calculation. On these points it was impossible to excel, or even to equal, Moreau'.

Jean-Victor-Marie Moreau in the uniform of a general – a portrait dating from his most successful period. A captured British officer entertained by Moreau in 1794 found him affable, 'pleasant and gay', a generous host at dinner, and very restrained in his dress, wearing a plain coat and an ordinary brass-hilted sword with a plain black knot. (Engraving by H.B.Hall after Guérin)

Charles Pichegru (1761–1804), a successful general of the early Revolutionary Wars, notably in the occupation of Holland. He was an opponent of the more extreme form of Republican government, however, and was exiled in 1797 as a consequence of his intrigues. As a Breton and the son of a man judicially murdered during the Terror, Moreau was bound to have an ambivalent attitude towards his predecessor's activities. Pichegru returned to France in 1803 as a leader of the planned insurrection, but was betrayed and arrested; he died in prison, probably by his own hand. (Engraving by W.Greatbatch)

Moreau at a later stage in his career. During his brief return to military service following his defection to Russia he was much esteemed by the Tsar, at whose side he was riding when mortally wounded at Dresden. It is said that the fatal roundshot was fired upon Napoleon's instruction when he noticed the group of enemy staff officers in conference. Moreau's greatest victory is commemorated by Thomas Campbell's well-known poem, *Hohenlinden*. (Engraving by C.State after J.L.Barbier-Walbonne)

However, if the two generals had approached each other from a hundred leagues' distance, 'the Emperor would have routed his adversary three, four, or five times over, before the latter could have had time to look about him'[38].

Moreau also lacked political judgment, and his ambitious wife encouraged his association with known malcontents. While unwilling to countenance Royalist intrigue, he remained an advocate of a Republic and was perhaps prepared to imagine himself as its head, if it could be restored. Relations with Napoleon had always been cool (the latter was known to favour his own lieutenants over those, like Bernadotte, who had served under Moreau); and although Moreau was not involved in the Cadoudal-Pichegru conspiracy, Napoleon had him arrested and banished for complicity. From 1804 to 1812 Moreau lived at Morrisville, New Jersey, USA, until upon Bernadotte's recommendation he agreed to return to Europe as military adviser to the Tsar. This aroused the enmity of his countrymen – Marbot, for example, described him as the new Coriolanus whose hatred of Napoleon led him to forget his country – but his revived military career was short-lived. At Dresden Moreau was dreadfully injured by a roundshot; he survived the amputation of both legs, calmly smoking a cigar throughout, but died five days later (2 September 1813) after he had been exhausted by attending a council of war. He was buried at St Petersburg, and his wife received a Russian pension. An early comment stated that 'his manners were simple, unaffected, and pure to a degree seldom found in French officers. Humane, generous, and beloved by his comrades'[39]. His career was essentially unsuccessful, however, and in his native country his laurels were tarnished by his having joined the enemy.

MORTIER, Maréchal Edouard-Adolphe-Casimir-Joseph, Duc de Trévise (1768–1835)

Known by Napoleon's punning nickname as 'the big mortar', Edouard Mortier (**see Plate I**) was among the most popular, honest and honourable of the marshals, and was also unusual in being an English-speaker. The son of a Cateau-Cambrécis cloth merchant and his English wife, he was educated at the English College at Douai and spent some time in Britain as a young man. Instead of the business career for which he had been intended, he joined the National Guard and was elected as an officer in his uncle's 1er Bn, Volontaires du Nord. Popular and imposing in build (he was the tallest of the marshals), he demonstrated his military talents in the early campaigns, and following distinguished service under Massena in Switzerland he became provisional *général de division* in September 1799, confirmed in the following month, only seven months after his promotion to *général de brigade*. An able administrator and a loyal follower of Napoleon, in 1804 he was among the first creation of the marshalate, and was appointed colonel-general of the Artillery and Seamen of the Imperial Guard.

In 1805 he won the action of Dürrenstein; succeeded Lannes in command of V Corps after Austerlitz; led VIII Corps in 1806–07, and commanded the left wing at Friedland. In July 1808 he was ennobled as Duke of Treviso (north of Venice). In the early Peninsular War he led V Corps and played an important part under Soult in the victories of Oçana and (conducting the battle himself) Gebora. He led the Young Guard in Russia in 1812, where he was appointed governor of Moscow;

Edouard-Adolphe-Casimir-Joseph Mortier, Duc de Trévise, in the full dress of a marshal – see Plate I1. The background figures can be seen in the original to be gunners, and a *marin* of the Imperial Guard, with an anchor and a pontoon bridge. They refer to Mortier's appointment as *Colonel-Général* of the Artillery and Seamen of the Guard – thus his aiguillette. Mortier has also been portrayed in this role wearing a uniform based upon that of the Artillerie à Cheval of the Guard. (Print by Lacoste & Moraine)

and commanded the Guard in the campaigns of 1813–14 where, like the Guard itself, he steadfastly clung to his duty in circumstances which others considered hopeless. After accepting a command from the king after the First Restoration, unlike others he remained loyal until the king had quit the country before returning to Napoleon's side.

It was intended that he should lead the Young Guard in the Hundred Days campaign, but severe sciatica prevented him from serving, his absence from this campaign proving a severe loss to Napoleon. Upon the Second Restoration he was only briefly in disgrace, and back in service as early as January 1816, although his titles and honours were not restored until 1819. In succeeding years he held a number of important posts, including ambassador to Russia, and president of the council and minister of war (1834–35). He was especially close to King Louis Philippe, whom he had met during the campaigns of 1792–93; and it was at his side that Mortier died, killed by the terrorist Fieschi's musket-battery device at the king's review of the National Guard on 28 July 1835. It was a trivial end for one who had survived countless battles, in the course of which he had gained a reputation as a competent subordinate commander, and more importantly as a modest, honourable man.

VICTOR, Maréchal Claude (Perrin), Duc de Bellune (1764–1841)

Although not one of the brightest stars in the Napoleonic firmament, Victor (**see Plate F**) was, as the emperor himself said, a rather better general than might have been imagined. Born in the Vosges of rather modest background, Claude Victor Perrin (who called himself Victor) joined the French artillery in 1781 but left after ten years to become a grocer. Only months later he re-entered military service with the Valence National Guard, and rose rapidly: a field officer within a year, he came to Napoleon's attention at Toulon, and after service in the Pyrenees and Italy became provisional *général de division* in January 1797, confirmed that March.

He commanded the left at Marengo with considerable distinction, but was sub-sequently employed in rather lesser positions, including commander of the Batavian army, minister to Denmark, and as Lannes' chief of staff in 1806. Captured by Prussian cavalry in January 1807 while commanding X Corps, he was transferred after exchange to I Corps, and sufficiently distinguished himself at Friedland finally to win his appoint-ment of marshal (13 July 1807). That August he became governor of Berlin. In September 1808 he received the title of Duke of Belluno (another town north of Venice) – not Marengo, as he had wished – a title said to have originated as a joke by Pauline Bonaparte. Victor's nickname was *'le beau soleil'*, supposedly from his sunny disposition; the reverse was the pun *'belle lune'*, transforming 'handsome sun' into 'beautiful moon'.

His next service, in Spain, brought mixed fortunes: victory at Espinosa and Medellin, but defeat at Talavera and Barrosa. He was recalled early in 1812 to command IX Corps in the Russian campaign, initially

operating in the army's rear but subsequently with great effect at the Berezina, where he helped keep open the route of retreat for the survivors of the Grande Armée – Napoleon remarked that he had performed with great credit. In the following year Victor led II Corps at Dresden and Leipzig, but on 18 February 1814 he was relieved of command on account of dilatory behaviour before Montereau. Though condemning his conduct, when Napoleon was faced with Victor's assertion that he was prepared to return to his military roots and fight as a private if necessary, he gave him command of two Young Guard provisional divisions, with which he was wounded at Craonne.

After his recovery Victor embraced the Bourbon restoration and never wavered from his new allegiance, attempting to rally resistance to Napoleon's return in 1815 and accompanying the king to Ghent during the Hundred Days. His loyalty was rewarded with the rank of major-general of the Royal Guard; he presided over a commission which investigated the conduct of officers during the late campaign, and voted for the death sentence at Ney's trial. He continued to hold important military positions (including minister of war 1821–23) until the revolution of 1830, when he retired after some 49 years' military service.

Mortier in the later stage of his career; the baton bearing stars rather than eagles, just visible beside his hat at low left, was a pattern introduced by King Louis-Philippe. Somewhat ungenerously, Napoleon once remarked that Mortier was the least effective of his marshals, but he was a capable subordinate and a man of unquestioned probity. Having survived two wounds on the battlefield, he had the unenviable distinction of being the last of Napoleon's marshals to die violently when he fell victim to a terrorist's 'infernal device' during an attempt on King Louis-Philippe's life in July 1835. (Engraving by E.Heinemann after N.M.Ponce-Camus)

Claude Victor (born Perrin), Duc de Bellune. Although his varied fortunes in the Peninsular War are well known, from the victories of Espinosa and Medellin to the defeat of Barrosa, his most valuable services to Napoleon were performed at Marengo and, notably, the Berezina.

BIBLIOGRAPHY

The following is in no way comprehensive, but lists significant works of value for further reading, including English-language biographies of personalities featured in this book, and others of more general or biographical interest. The emphasis has been placed upon titles in English.

Anon., *The Court and Camp of Bonaparte*, London 1831

Barton, Sir Dunbar P., *Bernadotte, the First Phase 1763–99; Bernadotte and Napoleon 1799–1810; Bernadotte, Prince and King 1810-44*, London 1914, 1921 & 1925

Bucquoy, E.L. (ed. LtCol Bucquoy & G.Devautour) *Les Uniformes du Premier Empire* – individual volumes: *Dragons et Guides*, Paris 1980 (includes the Guides of the Marshals); *Etat-Major et Service de Santé*, Paris 1982; *La Maison de l'Empéreur*, Paris 1984 (includes staff uniform and personalities)

Chandler, D.G., *The Campaigns of Napoleon*, London 1967.

Chandler, D.G., *Dictionary of the Napoleonic Wars*, London 1979

Chandler, D.G. (ed.), *Napoleon's Marshals*, London 1987

De Lisle, Gen H. de B., 'Great Cavalry Leaders: Lasalle', in *Cavalry Journal*, Vol.VII, 1912

Dewes, S., *Sergeant Belle-Jambe*, London 1934 (biography of Bernadotte)

Elting, J.R., *Swords Around a Throne: Napoleon's Grande Armée*, London 1989 (covers all aspects of Napoleon's army – an important study)

Gallagher, J.G., *The Iron Marshal: a Biography of Louis N. Davout*, Champaign, Illinois, 1976

Griffith, P., *The Art of War in Revolutionary France*, London 1998

Haythornthwaite, P.J., *Who was Who in the Napoleonic Wars*, London 1998

Horricks, R., *In Flight with the Eagle: a Guide to Napoleon's Elite*, Tunbridge Wells, 1988

Las Cases, Marquis de, *Memoirs of the Life, Exile and Conversations of the Emperor Napoleon*, London 1834

Lejeune, L.F., *Memoirs of Baron Lejeune: Aide-de-Camp to Marshals Berthier, Davout and Oudinot*, trans. Mrs A.Bell, London 1897

Linck, T., *Napoleon's Generals: The Waterloo Campaign*, Chicago, n.d.

Malibran, H., *Guide... des Uniformes de l'Armée français*, Paris 1904

Marbot, J.B.A.M., *The Memoirs of Baron de Marbot*, trans. A.J. Butler, London 1913

Marshall-Cornwall, Gen Sir James, *Massena*, Oxford 1965

Ojala, J.A., *Auguste de Colbert*, Salt Lake City 1979

Personal reconnaissance. Frederick the Great remarked on the importance of a general observing the terrain and the enemy dispositions in person: 'Everything should be examined by our own eyes, and no attentions of this nature treated on any account as matters of indifference'. Here General Moreau and his chief of staff make their own observations, escorted by only two hussars. (Print after Meissonier)

Palmer, A., *Bernadotte*, London 1990

Philippart, Sir John, *Memoirs of General Moreau*, London 1814

Phipps, R.W., *The Armies of the First French Republic and the Rise of the Marshals of Napoleon I*, Oxford 1926–39

Pigeard, A., *Les Etoiles de Napoléon*, Entremont-le-Vieux 1996 (illustrated biographical work on French marshals, generals and admirals 1792–1815)

Russell, Lord (of Liverpool), *Bernadotte, Marshal of France and King of Sweden*, London 1981

Sheppard, E.W., 'The Napoleonic Cavalry and its Leaders', in *Cavalry Journal*, Vols.XX–XXI, 1930–31

Six, G., *Dictionnaire Biographique des Généraux & Amiraux Français de la Révolution et de l'Empire 1792–1814*, Paris 1934 (an invaluable and minutely detailed reference)

Watson, S.J., *By Command of the Emperor: A Life of Marshal Berthier*, London 1957

Watson, S.J., *Carnot 1753–1823*, London 1954

Willing, P., *Napoléon et ses Soldats: l'Apogée de la Gloire 1804–1809*, Paris 1986

Zins, R., *Les Maréchaux du Premier Empire*, Paris n.d.

SOURCE NOTES

Abbreviated references refer to entries in the Bibliography.

(1) *Military Instruction from the Late King of Prussia to his Generals*, ed. T.Foster, London 1818, p.150

(2) *Tales from the Wars, or Naval & Military Chronicle*, Vol.II (2 December 1837), p.391

(3) Las Cases, Vol.I, p.189

(4) ibid

(5) Macdonald, J.E.J.A., *Recollections of Marshal Macdonald*, ed. C.Rousset, trans. S.L.Simeon, London 1892, Vol.II, pp.84–5

(6) Las Cases, Vol.IV, pp.109–10

(7) *Court & Camp*, p.242

(8) ibid, p.241

(9) Las Cases, Vol.I, p.341

(10) ibid

(11) ibid, p.342

(12) ibid, Vol.II, p.190

(13) ibid, pp.260–1

(14) *United Service Journal* 1843, Vol.I, p.577

(15) Lejeune, Vol.I, p.115

(16) Steevens, C., *Reminiscences of my Military Life*, ed. C.Steevens, Winchester 1878

(17) Ségur, P. de, *History of the Expedition to Russia*, London 1825, Vol.I, p.321

(18) *British Military Library or Journal*, London 1802, Vol.II, p.422

(19) *Monthly Review*, London 1804, p.541

(20) Las Cases, Vol.I, p.148

(21) Coignet, J.R., *The Note-Books of Captain Coignet*, ed. Sir John Fortescue, London 1928, p.178

(22) Las Cases, pp.338–9

(23) *Cavalry Journal*, Vol.XXI (1931), pp.96–7

(24) Las Cases, Vol.I, pp.391, 393

(25) Lejeune, Vol.I, p.128

(26) Las Cases, Vol.II, p.394

(27) ibid, Vol.I, pp.148, 251

(28) *Gentleman's Magazine*, July 1809, p.678

(29) Las Cases, Vol.I, p.251; Vol.II, pp.395–6

(30) Marbot, pp.381, 383

(31) Beamish, L., *History of the King's German Legion*, London 1832–7, Vol.I, p.360

(32) Las Cases, Vol.I, pp.189, 252

(33) Lejeune, Vol.I, p.271

(34) Marbot, p.483

(35) Stanhope, Earl, *Notes on Conversations with the Duke of Wellington*, London 1888, p.20

(36) Bunbury, Sir Henry, *Memoirs and Literary Remains of Lieutenant-General Sir Henry Edward Bunbury Bt.*, ed. Sir Charles Bunbury, London 1868, p.295

(37) Las Cases, Vol.I, p.251; Vol.II, p.356

(38) ibid, Vol.II, p.357

(39) *Court & Camp*, p.250

THE PLATES

A1: Général Adam-Philippe Custine, c1792
A2: Général Napoleon Bonaparte, c1796
A3: Général François-Christophe Kellermann, c1796
The figures of these three commanders from the French Revolutionary Wars illustrate the changes in the uniform of general officers. Originally their uniform was an amendment of that of 1786, including a gold-laced dark blue coat. The everyday *petit uniforme* is shown in the figure of **Custine**, taken from a portrait. The rank of *lieutenant-général* was shown by the double line of lace on the cuff (one for *maréchal de camp*), and four on the pockets; the dress coat had a standing collar, and no lapels or cuff-flaps. White waistcoat and breeches replaced the scarlet of 1786, and although the hat officially had black silk edging for *petit uniforme* this is sometimes shown with the gold-laced dress hat.

The 1794 uniform, as in the figure of **Kellermann** (also from a portrait), introduced scarlet collar and cuffs and gold oak-leaf embroidery (a double row for *général de division*) and white cuff-flaps (apparently missing in the Kellermann portrait). The sash for *général en chef*, ordered in 1796, was red and white with a gold fringe, and a tricolour feather panache was ordered for the hat, but is absent from the Kellermann portrait.

The 1796 uniform is shown in the figure of **Bonaparte**, taken from a portrait by Gros: coloured as before but single-breasted, with embroidery down the front for *général en chef* only, and less embroidery for a *général de brigade* than for *de division*. A *général en chef* wore the red and white sash and a red plume with a tricolour panache; *général de division*, a scarlet sash with tricolour fringe and a tricolour plume with red panache; and *général de brigade*, a sky-blue sash with tricolour fringe, and tricolour plume and panache – although contemporary pictures show a number of variations to these regulations.

B1: Général Thomas-Alexandre Dumas (Davy de la Pailleterie)
B2: Officer, Bonaparte's Guides (Nicolas Dahlmann)
B3: Général Jean-Baptiste Kléber
These three personalities were associated with the campaign in Egypt. In August 1798 a double-breasted coat for general officers was re-introduced, in the same colours. For a *général de division* it bore a double row of embroidery on collar, cuffs and pockets, and was worn with a red sash and a blue and white plume over a red panache; the same for *général en chef*, with a red, white and blue sash and a white plume with blue base; and for *général de brigade*, a single row of embroidery, sky-blue sash, and white and red plume over a blue panache. A gold-embroidered shoulder-belt could also be worn for ceremonial occasions: white with red edge for *général en chef*, red for *général de division* and sky blue for *de brigade*.

The figure of **Kléber** is taken from a portrait, evidently showing the earlier pattern of sash for *général en chef*, with all-red hat feathers, and a mameluke sabre suspended on a shoulder cord, a popular style among those serving in Egypt. **Dumas** is shown in the 1796 uniform of *général de division*, with the 1796-regulation plumes and sash. The **officer of Bonaparte's Guides** depicts the uniform of this small escort unit, formed in September 1796 and ultimately

François-Christophe Kellermann wearing the *petit uniforme* of 1791, bearing the double line of lace around the cuffs which indicated the rank of *lieutenant-général*. The lace used at this period resembled a folded ribbon with an uneven edge, very different from the gold oak-leaf embroidery which succeeded it. In the original the hat plume is white with a red tip and blue base. (Engraving by G.Wolf after H.Rouget)

expanded to incorporate infantry and artillery as well as the original cavalry. The green chasseur uniform (from a painting by Lejeune) was the origin of that of the Chasseurs à Cheval of the Imperial Guard, into which the unit evolved.

The figure represents Nicolas Dahlmann (1769–1807), who had served as an ordinary soldier in the cavalry of the Ancien Régime and rose through the ranks of the Guides de Bonaparte to attain a captaincy in Egypt. He became colonel-major of the Chasseurs à Cheval of the Guard after service at Austerlitz, where his predecessor, Morland, was killed. (Napoleon ordered that the latter's body be taken home to be buried in style, but it was stored in a barrel of spirits and forgotten for some years, until the barrel decayed, whereupon Morland's family had to prevent the preserved remains from becoming a scientific exhibit.) Dahlmann became *général de brigade* in December 1806, but was wounded by a shot in the thigh at Eylau, and died two days later.

The young General Bonaparte – cf Plate A2. He was appointed provisionally as *général de brigade* in December 1793, and confirmed in that rank the following February; and provisionally as *général de division* in October 1795, confirmed the following March. Since he had been commissioned as an officer in 1785 his rise to high rank was in fact somewhat slower than that of some of those who were later his subordinates. (Engraving by R.G.Tietze after J.A.Rouillard)

C1: Général Louis-Charles-Antoine Desaix
C2: ADC to Général de Division
C3: Napoleon Bonaparte, 1800

The figure of **Desaix** shows the uniform of *général de division*, with the double line of embroidery indicative of rank on collar and cuffs; the red plume and tricolour panache, taken from a contemporary painting, are a variation on the regulation. Portraits of Desaix in Egypt show a mameluke sabre carried on a shoulder cord in local style, and one depicts a dark blue, civilian-style coat devoid of military features.

The **general's ADC** illustrated wears the uniform prescribed for that appointment: a dark blue *surtout* with sky blue facings, and a brassard around the upper arm to identify the rank of general whom the ADC served: white, red or blue for *en chef*, *de division* and *de brigade* respectively. The plume shown is the regulation one for *général de division*, though the contemporary painting from which the remainder of the figure is taken shows a non-regulation yellow plume.

The figure of **Napoleon** is based upon Lejeune's picture of Marengo and upon the coat he wore at the battle. Lejeune

also shows the use of a light grey overcoat, and no sash – perhaps because, as First Consul, Napoleon was prohibited officially from commanding troops in the field (although he did, of course).

D1: Général Jean-Marie-Pierre-François
  Lepaige Dorsenne
D2: Maréchal Louis-Nicolas Davout
D3: Général Pierre-Auguste Hulin

This plate illustrates personalities associated with the Imperial Guard, all of whom are included in the biographical section. The figure of **Dorsenne**, based partly upon a portrait, wears the uniform of the Grenadiers à Pied of the Guard, with the distinctions of *général de division*: a double row of gold oak-leaf embroidery on collar and cuffs, sash with interwoven red lines, and the three silver stars of rank (*général de brigade* used two) on the knot of the sash, epaulettes and sword-knot. His decorations include the Légion d'Honneur (red ribbon), the Order of the Iron Crown of the Kingdom of Italy (yellow ribbon with green edges) and the Order of Military Merit of Maximilian Joseph of Bavaria (white enamelled cross with black ribbon with white and blue edges).

French general and officer, San Domingo: watercolour by J.A.Langendyk, dated 1802 – cf Plate B1. A number of French generals were born in the colonies, including San Domingo, which was the scene of much hard campaigning. Although the best-known was the remarkable Toussaint L'Ouverture other important generals from that island included André Rigaud (1761–1811), a soldier of some ability who had served in the American War of Independence. The general depicted here has plumes of red, white and blue. (The Royal Collection © 2000 HM Queen Elizabeth II)

The figure of **Davout**, based upon a contemporary portrait and a preserved coat, shows the dress uniform of a marshal, with the gold aiguillette which was a distinction of the Imperial Guard, worn by Davout by virtue of his appointment in 1804 as Colonel-General of the Grenadiers à Pied of the Guard. Marshals' coats were blue throughout, and bore gold oak-leaf embroidery in varied quantities, as shown in other plates. The sash, like that of a *général en chef*, was made of gold fabric with white interwoven, and bore the device of a marshal upon the knot of the tassel: crossed batons, which were also borne upon the epaulettes and buttons. Davout's decorations include the scarlet sash with enamelled badge at the knot, the medal and (upper) breast star of the Légion d'Honneur, and the (lower) breast star of the Portuguese Order of Christ, which he received in 1806.

In September 1803 a new uniform was ordered for general officers and worn for the remainder of the period. The coat was single-breasted, and bore a double row of oak-leaf embroidery on the collar and cuffs for *général de division*, and a single row for *général de brigade*, as here. The ranks were also differentiated by the coloured lines woven into the gold sash: scarlet for *général de division*, light blue for *de brigade*. Early hand-coloured prints often have slight variations; in this example the breeches appear grey, but are intended to be white. The orderly is evidently a trooper of the 9e Hussards: red dolman, light blue facings and breeches, yellow lace, and a dark green shako plume tipped with yellow. (Print by Martinet)

General Charles-Victor-Emmanuel Leclerc (1772–1802). In this posthumous portrait he wears a coat similar to that of 1803, with the embroidered *baudrier* of a *général en chef* (see also on page 60 in portrait of Napoleon as First Consul). Leclerc was Napoleon's brother-in-law, married to Pauline Bonaparte. He saw extensive service during the Revolutionary Wars, but is most remembered for commanding the French army on San Domingo, where he died of fever some ten months after his arrival. The announcement of his death described him as 'at once a hero and a sage. He had dignity without pride, generosity without ostentation; his heart was right'. (Engraving by M.Haider after F.Kinson)

The figure of **Hulin** is also taken from a portrait, showing an undress version of the uniform of a *général de division*. Generals' dress or *grand uniforme* was embroidered in a similar way to that illustrated, but with skirts not turned back; and there was a plainer version which bore the embroidery only upon collar and cuffs.

E1: Général Jean-Andoche Junot
E2: Louis Bonaparte, King of Holland
E3: Maréchal André Massena
The figure of **Junot** displays the uniform of Colonel-General of Hussars, an appointment Junot received in July 1804. A number of differing features are shown in depictions of this

Napoleon as First Consul, in the gold-embroidered scarlet uniform and white waistcoat of that civil appointment. However, note the details of the gold-embroidered white *baudrier* or shoulder-belt, which is similar to that worn on ceremonial occasions by general officers. (Print after Appiani)

uniform: this is based upon an illustration by Isabey, showing the white dolman with red facings, blue pelisse and breeches, with gold generals' oak-leaf embroidery on the collar and cuffs; others show plain gold lace edging. Other versions appear to show a white and gold barrelled sash, and Gros depicts the raquettes hanging on the opposite side of the shako. The ribbon is that of the Légion d'Honneur, with the breast star and medal of that order, and the medal of the Order of the Iron Crown, on the pelisse.

The figure of **Louis Bonaparte** is based upon a portrait by Charles Hodges, showing the characteristic white uniform of the army of the Kingdom of Holland; the blue ribbon is that of the Royal Order of Merit, founded by Louis in 1806.

The figure of **Massena** is based upon a portrait by Gros, showing the full dress of a marshal, similar to that in Plate D2; a marked variation is the design of eagles upon the knots of the tassels of the sash. The decorations are all those of the Légion d'Honneur. Massena carries the baton of a marshal, which had gilt ferrules and bore gold eagles upon its dark blue covering.

F1: Général Géraud-Christophe-Michel Duroc, as Grand Marshal of the Palace
F2: Maréchal Claude Victor (Perrin)
F3: Maréchal Charles-Pierre-François Augereau

The dress of a marshal included a *grand uniforme*, a very rich version of the dress coat, usually velvet, with elaborate gold embroidery of oak-leaf design carried on the shoulder seams of the sleeve, on the sleeve seams and on the rear; its buttons might also be covered with gold-embroidered velvet. This coat could form part of a 'court dress' or *grand costume de gala* which, on the most ceremonial occasions, could be worn with a cape and hat with immense plumes. The figures of **Augereau** and **Victor** in this plate, taken from portraits by Lefevre and Gros respectively, both wear this uniform; Victor carries the short-bladed sword of imitation classical style, sometimes termed a 'glaive', which was carried on ceremonial occasions by marshals and the holders of some offices of state. A similarly magnificent court dress was worn by ministers and those holding important offices: an example is the scarlet uniform worn here by **Duroc** as Grand Marshal of the Palace, from a portrait by Gros. The sash and various badges of the Légion d'Honneur are displayed prominently, including upon the cape.

G1: Général Jean-Joseph Ange, Comte d'Hautpoul
G2: Général Antoine-Charles-Louis Lasalle
G3: Colonel-Major Louis Lepic

This plate shows three cavalry commanders distinguished during the campaigns of 1806–07, all of whom are featured in the biographical section. **Hautpoul** is shown in the uniform of a cuirassier general, with the general officer's coat worn in conjunction with the helmet and cuirass of that arm of service, with the sash of *général de division* worn over the cuirass, and the Légion d'Honneur affixed to its shoulder-scale.

Lasalle is shown in campaign uniform as *général de brigade*, from a portrait by Gros; other portraits in more formal uniform show scarlet breeches and hussar boots. The pelisse is worn over a braided waistcoat, its raquettes bearing the two silver rank stars of *général de brigade*, which were also carried on the sabretache. The loose trousers with false boots were so identified with him that the style was given the term 'à la Lasalle'; another item associated with this flamboyant hussar was a large pipe, which he smoked even in battle.

Lepic is shown wearing the regimental headdress of the Grenadiers à Cheval of the Guard, and a braided coat or pelisse of unregulated pattern, which contemporary paintings show were worn quite widely in the winter campaign.

H1: Joseph-François Bernadotte
H2: Maréchal Jean-Baptiste-Jules Bernadotte
H3: ADC to Bernadotte

The figure of **Marshal Bernadotte** is taken from a portrait by Kinson, showing the dress uniform of a marshal; although it does not bear the maximum amount of embroidery worn for occasions of great ceremony, the original painting appears to indicate that the coat is made of velvet. The ribbon and decorations are those of the Légion d'Honneur, with the lower breast star of the Order of the Black Eagle of Prussia, which Bernadotte received in 1805.

In addition to the regulated uniform of aides-de-camp, it was the custom for the personal staffs of marshals to wear a

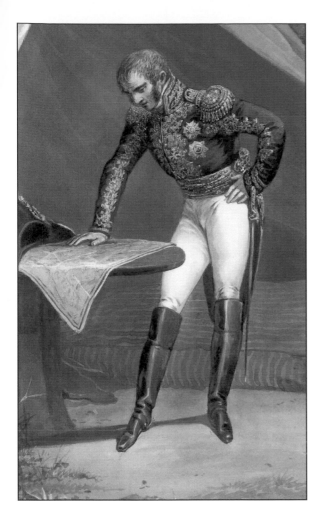

The elegance of the most richly embroidered *grand uniforme* version of the marshal's coat is shown in this watercolour by Alexander I.Sauerweid dated 1816 – cf Plate F3. There appears to be an error in the depiction of the rank insignia, however: the epaulettes bear the three silver stars of a *général de division* rather than the crossed batons of a marshal. (The Royal Collection © 2000 HM Queen Elizabeth II)

uniform unique to themselves, an example of which is shown in the other figures on this plate. The uniform of Bernadotte's ADCs was recorded by the so-called 'Bourgeois of Hambourg' (the brothers Christian and Cornelius Suhr), who documented the uniforms of troops observed in Hamburg, 1806–14. Three different uniforms are shown for Bernadotte's aides during his governorship of the Hanseatic region. Their magnificent full dress consisted of a chamois dolman with lightish blue facings and gold lace, chamois pelisse, lightish blue or chamois breeches laced gold, hussar boots (shown by Suhr as either red or yellow), and a busby with chamois bag.

This uniform is substantially that shown here as worn by **Bernadotte's son Joseph-François** (1799–1859), who with his mother joined the marshal at Hamburg – and who was to succeed his father as King Oscar I of Sweden upon

Bernadotte's death on 8 March 1844. Suhr shows the young boy wearing a uniform of his father's aides, even including the white brassard which identified the ADC of a marshal, but with a shako instead of the busby. The red sabretache with gold lace and eagle device was evidently the 'dress' version of the black leather pattern carried by the **ADC shown as H3**, who wears what may have been the 'ordinary' uniform of Bernadotte's staff – medium-blue hussar uniform with chamois facings. A third uniform was the undress: a chasseur coat and breeches in the same medium blue with chamois facings, worn with a white waistcoat, hussar boots and bicorn hat.

I1: Maréchal Adolphe-Edouard-Casimir-Joseph Mortier
I2: Trooper, Mortier's Guides
I3: Trooper, Bernadotte's Guides
Mortier is shown in the uniform of a marshal, with the addition of the Imperial Guard aiguillette, signifying his appointment as Colonel-General of the Artillery and Seamen of the Guard. The decorations are those of the Légion d'Honneur, with the medal of the Order of the Iron Crown, and the (lower) breast star of the Order of Christ of Portugal, which he received in 1806. This also illustrates the horse-furniture of a marshal, including a crimson shabraque and holster-caps with gold lace and fringe edging, and a gold imperial crown in the rear corners.

In addition to their aides, some marshals maintained small units of headquarters Guides dressed in distinctive uniforms. Mortier formed his Guides in June 1803 while he was governor of Hanover; they were dressed originally in chasseur uniform. In 1806, when given command of VIII Corps of the Grande Armée, his escort was dressed in the striking yellow and green **hussar uniform shown as I2**, based upon an illustration by Weiland. The braid appears to have been mixed green and yellow; unusually the busby has a brass, crowned eagle badge, and the plumes are also recorded as either dark green, or green over black.

Bernadotte's Guides were formed when he succeeded Mortier as governor of Hanover in May 1804; their red and green hussar uniform apparently changed in some minor aspects. **Figure I3** is based upon an illustration by the 'Bourgeois of Hambourg', c1806–07, which shows lace of a reddish colour, possibly intended to be *amaranth*, but perhaps more likely to be *aurore* if, as seems possible, the uniform were copied from that of the Chasseurs à Cheval of the Imperial Guard with the colours of pelisse and dolman reversed. Another illustration shows what was presumably winter dress, with a red-braided green pelisse worn as a jacket, and green overall trousers; Suhr's other figures have white plumes. The earlier uniform is shown in a portrait by Lefevre, which includes a red plume, mixed green and white lace, and lace knots on the thighs.

J1: Maréchal Jean-Baptiste Bessières
J2: Général Auguste-François-Marie de Colbert
J3: Général Charles Lefebvre-Desnouettes
This plate shows three of Napoleon's cavalry commanders who were engaged in the early part of the Peninsular War. The figure of **Bessières**, based on a portrait by Riesener, depicts the uniform of Colonel-General of the cavalry of the Imperial Guard, including the green chasseur-style coat of the Chasseurs à Cheval of the Guard, with scarlet waistcoat

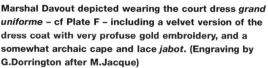

Marshal Davout depicted wearing the court dress *grand uniforme* – cf Plate F – including a velvet version of the dress coat with very profuse gold embroidery, and a somewhat archaic cape and lace *jabot*. (Engraving by G.Dorrington after M.Jacque)

Jean-Baptiste Bessières in the uniform of *Colonel-Général* of the cavalry of the Imperial Guard – see Plate J1. The green chasseur-style coat of the Guard Chasseurs à Cheval is worn with a gold-laced red waistcoat and breeches. (Engraving by C.State after Reisener)

and breeches, the Guard aiguillette, the sash of a marshal and a mameluke-style sabre. The decorations are those of the Légion d'Honneur, with the lower breast star of the Portuguese Order of Christ, which he was awarded in 1806.

The figure of **Colbert** is taken from a portrait by Gérard, which shows a very plain campaign or undress coat decorated only with epaulettes, with the sash of *général de brigade* (gold with interwoven blue lines) and a white-plumed hat; the medals are those of the Légion d'Honneur and the Order of the Iron Crown. Like Bessières, **Lefebvre-Desnouettes** also wears a uniform of the Chasseurs à Cheval of the Guard, though in the alternative hussar style; he was colonel-major of the regiment. The silver stars of his rank as *général de division* are carried on the raquettes of the busby and pelisse; the breast star worn on the pelisse was that of the Order of Fidelity of Baden, which he had received in 1807. At Benavente he was recorded as wearing a much plainer uniform, including what was described as a green 'frock' (presumably the green chasseur-style coat of his regiment) and a cocked hat.

K1: Maréchal Louis-Alexandre Berthier
K2: Louis-François Lejeune, ADC to Berthier
K3: ADC to Berthier

Napoleon's devoted chief of staff **Berthier** is shown here in a common campaign uniform for marshals and general officers: a plain coat or *frac* with embroidery of rank on the collar and cuffs only, and in this case the aiguillette which he wore as Major-General of the Grande Armée.

Berthier was another who dressed his ADCs in a distinctive uniform, designed by one of them, Louis-François Lejeune (1775–1848), who first served Berthier in 1800, became Davout's chief of staff in I Corps in September 1812, and was promoted to *général de brigade* in the same month. Lejeune's most lasting fame, however, was as one of the leading battle painters of his generation. The uniform which Lejeune designed made Berthier's ADCs very distinctive: white dolman, black pelisse and scarlet shako, with gold lace. **Figure K2** is based upon a self-portrait by Lejeune, showing scarlet breeches; scarlet overalls with a black stripe were also worn, and other recorded variations include a black shako and facings. In full dress the ADCs rode grey horses with gold-decorated horse furniture and pantherskin shabraques edged with gold and scarlet, so that Lejeune recorded that when they paraded in Madrid at the head of the Guard he never saw anything so brilliant in appearance. On campaign the uniform had mixed advantages: by virtue of the red shako and trousers he was able to glean information from hostile civilians in the Peninsula by pretending to be British, even despite the eagle on his sabretache; but he noted that at Saragossa the red shako was dangerously conspicuous and drew enemy fire.

An alternative uniform for Berthier's ADCs is shown in **Figure K3**, including a red coat with black collar and cuffs and white lapels, cut in chasseur style and decorated with gold oak-leaf embroidery.

L1: Général de Brigade
L2: Maréchal Jean Lannes
L3: Colonel of Engineers (Guillaume Dode)

These figures are shown as they might have appeared at the siege of Saragossa in 1809. That of the anonymous **général de brigade** wears the common campaign uniform of the *frac* with simplified embroidery and two silver stars on the epaulettes; hat with black feather edging; and the sash with interwoven blue lines, indicative of this rank.

The figure of **Lannes** is based upon a portrait by Gérard, depicting the *petit uniforme* as it might be worn on campaign,

with the embroidered white shoulder-belt (*baudrier*) which was used to identify a *général en chef* but was probably reserved for ceremonial occasions. In addition to the star and medal of the Légion d'Honneur and the medal of the Order of the Iron Crown, the lower breast star is that of the Order of St Andrew of Russia, which he had received in 1807.

The **engineer officer** illustrates Colonel Guillaume Dode, Baron (later Vicomte) de la Brunerie (1775–1851), who represents one of the middle-ranking officers who rose to greatest prominence after the Napoleonic Wars. Commissioned in 1795, Dode commanded the engineers of Lannes' V Corps from 1806. He was the senior engineer officer to survive unscathed through the second siege of Saragossa, following the death of Général André-Bruno Lacoste and the wounding of Joseph Rogniat. Dode's engineer detachment of V Corps at the siege was only small (seven engineer officers, and three officers and 62 other ranks from No.5 company, 2e Bn de Sapeurs), but their importance in such operations was crucial. Dode became a *général de brigade* in March 1809, *lieutenant-général* in August 1814, and retained his rank under the Restoration despite having it confirmed by Napoleon in 1815. In 1847 he was appointed a Marshal of France, one of the few engineers to achieve that distinction. He is shown here wearing engineer uniform, with black velvet facings and red piping, and the blue breeches commonly worn on campaign.

Berthier's aides in their alternative uniform of a red chasseur-style coat with black facings, white lapels, gold oak-leaf embroidery, and the aiguillette worn as representatives of the *Major-Général* of the Grande Armée – see Plate K3. Although the colouring of this uniform was retained its cut was later changed to that of the 1812 regulations, with lapels closed to the waist and 'gauntlet' cuffs substituted for this pointed style. (Print after 'Job')

Lannes – see Plate L2 – at Aspern-Essling, following the amputation of his shattered right leg. Napoleon kneels beside his friend, almost overcome with emotion. Baron Larrey, who performed the operation, stands at left, while Bessières – no friend of Lannes – is recognisable in the background. (Print after E.Boutigny)

INDEX

Figures in **bold** refer to illustrations